TAKE HEART!

A WIDOWED MAN'S GUIDE TO GROWING STRONGER

Written by:

Bruce McLeod and

Rev. Chris Taylor

Scripture quotations taken from the *Amplified Bible* (AMPC), Copyright 1954, 1958, 1962, 1964, 1965, 1987 by The Lockman Foundation. Used by permission. *www.lockman.org*.

Scripture quotations marked (*CEV*) are from the *Contemporary English Version* 1991, 1992, 1995 by American Bible Society. Used by permission.

Scripture verses marked (KJV) are from the *King James Version of the Bible* (public domain).

Scripture quotations from *THE MESSAGE*. Eugene H. Peterson, copyright 1993, 1994, 1995, 1996, 2000, 2001, 2002. Used by permission of NavPress Publishing Group.

Scripture taken from the *New American Standard Bible* (NASB) 1960, 1962, 1968, 1971, 1973, 1975, 1977 by The Lockman Foundation. Used by permission.

Scripture quotations marked (NCV) are taken from the *New Century Version*. Copyright 1987, 1988, 1991 by Word Publishing, a division of Thomas Nelson, Inc. Used by permission. All rights reserved.

All Scripture quotations, unless otherwise indicated, are taken from the *Holy Bible, New International Version (*NIV*)*. Copyright 1973, 1978, 1984, by International Bible Society· Used by permission of Zondervan. All rights reserved·

Scripture quotations marked (NKJV) are taken from the *New King James Version*. Copyright 1982 by Thomas Nelson, Inc. Used by permission. All rights reserved.

Scripture quotations marked (*NLT*) are taken from the *Holy Bible, New Living Translation*, copyright 1996. Used by permission of Tyndale House Publishers, Inc. All rights reserved.

TAKE HEART!

I have told you these things, so that in Me you may have peace. In this world you will have trouble. But take heart! I have overcome the world (John 16:33).

I have told you these things, so that in Me you may have [perfect] peace and confidence. In the world you have tribulation and trials and distress and frustration; but be of good cheer [take courage; be confident, certain, undaunted]! For I have overcome the world. [I have deprived it of power to harm you and have conquered it for you.]   (John 16:33, AMPC).

You who suffer take heart. Christ is the answer to sorrow.[1]
Billy Graham

1   Worthy Inspired, *Overcoming Tough Times: God's Answer to Every Situation* (New York: Worthy Publishing), p. 208.

DEDICATION

We dedicate this work to Cheri and Irene.
They were our "one flesh," as God would have it.
They walked many miles with us upon our journey
to becoming more like Jesus.

TABLE OF CONTENTS

ACKNOWLEDGEMENTS

Many thanks to Rolland Wright,
founder of The Widows Project and
Mary Beth Woll, co-author of *Don't Lose Heart!*,
who challenged and inspired us to undertake this project.
We wouldn't have done it at all otherwise.

Thanks too for Mary Beth and Linda Smith's editing
suggestions and advice. You made the work more
understandable and applicable to our audience.

Many thanks to Sherry Esp, our proof reader,
who caught more mistakes, mis-speakings and unclarity
than we thought ourselves capable of making.

Great appreciation and thanks to Inger Logelin,
our chief editor, who made our words flow easily and sensibly.
What an artist!

A huge thank you to Kristi Knowles, our final editor and
amazing publisher, without whom this work would
not be printed.

Most importantly, thank You, Jesus,
for inspiring, encouraging, and strengthening us
throughout the process.
This work is our thank offering to You.
You are our life!

FOREWORD

It is with great honor that I make this contribution to the male companion of *Don't Lose Heart!* From the inception of the thought behind The Widows Project, I had the belief that a man's grief is every bit as profound as the grief women experience at the loss of a spouse. Observing Bruce over the past year and hearing other men express their grief via our various grief group options has only served to validate my assertion.

Take Heart! is an answer to prayer. I have prayed for proprietary grief products for the past seven years. God has dynamically answered this prayer with a male version of *Don't Lose Heart!*

I recall the day Bruce came onto our weekly online prayer call. He was the first on the call, so he announced to me that friends of his had prophetically told him, "You are going to be writing a book."

Without hesitation, I responded, "And I know what you are supposed to write—the male version of *Don't Lose Heart!*"

He hesitated for a moment, seemingly taken aback by my statement. It was as seamless as if we had rehearsed the lines. Because I had prayed for this outcome, I was prepared when I heard Bruce say it. I'm sure he was surprised, but I was not. The moment I heard those words come from his mouth, I knew this was the answer.

As an organization, we use 2 Corinthians 1:3–4 as our foundation. I can say unequivocally that Bruce and Chris are extending the comfort, compassion, and encouragement which God has given them.

Like the co-authors of *Don't Lose Heart!*, our *Take Heart!* co-authors are good and longtime friends. Together they have created a men's resource for helping men navigate the landmines of grief and loss. I know of no other group-processing resource available that comes from the personal walk of both authors so uniquely.

You would do well to provide a copy of this book to every man who, in loving well, is grieving deeply.

To the man who is receiving this book, I encourage you to process your grief in a group. Men tend to isolate, which compounds their grief and delays or slows down the healing process.

This book is an invaluable gift. Bruce and Chris are taking you by the hand and walking this journey with you. Together with the Holy Spirit, you could not be in better company.

Rolland Wright, Founder, The Widows Project

TAKE heart!

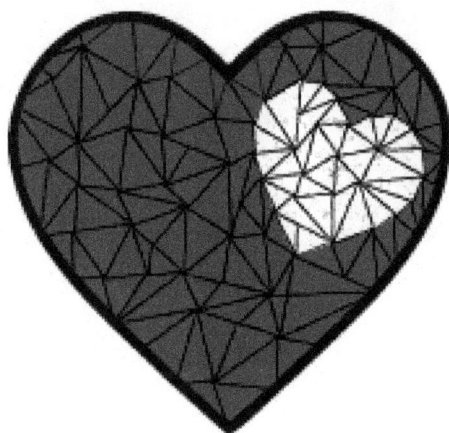

A WIDOWED MAN'S GUIDE TO GROWING STRONGER

BY REV. CHRIS TAYLOR AND BRUCE McLEOD

Keep First Things First

Develop an intimate relationship with Jesus because you are powerless to overcome grief in your own strength.

Chapter One

Keep First Things First

Develop an Intimate relationship with Jesus

The Lord is close to the brokenhearted
and saves those who are crushed in spirit
(Psalm 34:18).

When I (Bruce) first met Cheri in the fall of 1993, I did not want to take my eyes off her. I just couldn't get enough of her. I wanted to be with her every moment I could. I made excuses—to myself and others—for that to happen. I tried my best to weave her into every facet of my life. I'm not quite sure how I managed to also do my job at work, feed myself, and take care of my little home. My deep conviction is that God brought us together for some exceptionally good reasons. Even then, I had a fairly close relationship with Him. Through that relationship, I believe His Spirit empowered me to do all my work while courting Cheri.

Cheri and I did our level best to have a God-centered marriage, home, and family. We applied ourselves to this, learned, and grew to the extent that we were able to help others do the same. We continued this work until just a few weeks before her death.

Brokenhearted and Crushed

When Cheri passed away in December of 2017, I was left brokenhearted and crushed. I couldn't concentrate on much at all, and felt lost, helpless, and unable to connect with life. I remembered something a great friend once told me: "When bad stuff happens to me, I have a choice. I can run *to* God, or I can run *away* from Him." I had already proven for myself the futility of choice #2, so I purposed to run to God. I did not want to take the eyes of my heart off Him. I just couldn't get enough of Him. I wanted to be with Him every moment I could. I made excuses—to myself and others—for that to happen. I tried my best to weave Him into every facet of my life, developing new habits to empower that. I pursued intimacy with Him because I was powerless on my own to deal with the grief. And, wonder of wonders, He showed up! And boy, did He show off! He brought me peace in the midst of chaos. He brought me comfort beyond my imagining. He brought me sound counsel about what to do with myself. And He showed me how to deal with this new and so very different life.

§

For me (Chris) the words "comfort beyond my imagining" dropped into my heart and really impressed me. I gave my heart to Jesus shortly after Irene and I were married. For thirty-eight years, I had walked with Jesus. I never walked away from Him, and He never walked away from me. Even though we walked together, I didn't know how much more I would need Him. That started when my wife passed in December of 2010.

Three things helped me trust Jesus more than ever and gave me the comfort I desperately needed.

First, He reminded me of His great love for me. The day I made a commitment to Jesus, I was completely overwhelmed by a sense of His love as soon as I said, "Yes." I had never felt that kind of powerful and emotional love in my whole life, and it permeated me inside and out. For Jesus to die for me and to love me like that was beyond my imagining. *That* is comfort. I can trust a Jesus like *that*.

Second, I was reminded how consistent Jesus had been over the years. When He said, "I will never leave you," (Hebrews 13:5, NKJV), I found He actually meant it. Through all of life's ups and downs, He was always right beside me. He was doing life together with me. He was more consistent with me than I was with Him. When I found myself in that lonely place of grief, there He was, again and again, 24-hours a day. *That* is comfort. I can trust a Jesus like *that*.

Third, I remembered that He really understands me. He understands my feelings, my pain of loss, and the gut-wrenching sadness that filled my life in the early days of my grief journey. Isaiah 53:3 (NKJV), describes Jesus as "a man of sorrows and acquainted with grief," not just because He is God. After all, God knows everything. He knows because He has *experienced* those things. I'll take the guy with the experience over the guy with the theory anytime. I know Jesus knows, and that brings comfort beyond imagining to me. I can trust a Jesus like *that*.

My question is, "Can you trust Him as well?"

§

One day, early on in my grief journey, I (Bruce) was feeling lonely and anxious. I felt my life was in total chaos and out of control. I went weeping to Jesus, pouring out my heart to Him. I cried aloud all the feelings I felt swirling in my heart. Finally, I felt that well run dry. I asked the Lord that wonderful question we learned in GriefShare: "What comfort or counsel would you give me about all of this, Jesus?"

Through the "eyes of my heart," I "saw" an image of Jesus as my Shepherd. I was His sheep—an old ram with great curling horns. I was lying with my head in my Shepherd's lap. We reclined on a grassy hillside under a shade tree on a warm, sunny day. He was gazing deeply into my eyes with His eyes of pure love, and gently stroking my head in the space between my horns. He even caressed the horns themselves with His hands. Then He threw His arms around my neck, hugged me to Himself, and rolled us down the hill into the soft, warm grass. Both of us were laughing for the pure joy and fun of being together.

Following that experience, my heart was full of peace, thanksgiving, and joy. All that pain and chaos were gone—at least for a while. As I have pondered this since, I've received more and more understanding. I developed this affirmation of what Jesus did in my heart: "I have seen the timeline of my life. You showed me, Jesus, my Shepherd. You walked it with me—lamb to ram."

The Lord often uses imagery to speak to my heart. The Holy Spirit has often reminded me of this image over the ensuing years. Those reminders, sometimes more like re-livings of the experience, have always brought comfort and relief from the chaos of the moment and peace in the depths of my heart.

FIRST THINGS FIRST

If these stories concerning relationship with God seem strange to you, they needn't. You can have this same sort of comfort and intimacy, custom-made to suit your own needs. The starting point is offering your heart to Jesus. If you haven't before, but are now ready to start a personal relationship with Jesus, you might pray this prayer:

Jesus, You and I both know that I have messed up choices in life. I've done things at times that have hurt You and others. I believe You died on the cross and rose to life again to pay for my mistakes. I ask You right now to come into my heart

and become the Lord of my life. Forgive me for the mistakes
I have made in the past or may commit in the future. Amen.

Once you have done this, you are ready to make Him the Lord of
your life. Here are some of the habits I developed to keep my heart
focused on Him:

QUIET TIMES

During my grieving process, I've used early morning devotional
readings that center my heart, mind, and will on God. I've used
Jesus Calling: Enjoying Peace in His Presence by Sarah Young and
Every Mourning by Donna Fagerstrom.

CHECK-INS

Upon completing a task, or the day's portion of it, I stop for a
moment, maybe take a few deep breaths, and close my eyes. Then I
say something like this: "Thanks for getting me through that, Jesus.
What's next?" Then I listen with the "ears of my heart" for what He
might "speak" to me, and I open the "eyes of my heart" for what
He might "show" me. This practice gives me peace and liberates me
from the tyranny of my to-do lists.

WALKIE-TALKIES

I take two walks a day. My dog Duncan helps with this. Duncan
and I walk; God and I talk. Often, I use rote prayers to help me keep
my grief-scattered thoughts focused. I'll include a couple in the
Resources section at the end of the book.

JOURNALING

I have kept several journals. My *Get Today Journal* is a record
of my impressions from God. I daily ask Him, "What's the big deal
today? What do You want me to "get" from You today?" I record my
attempts to accomplish what I have been impressed to do.

Another journal I keep is of Scripture promises I have found
that feel right for me. This involves two journals: My *Promises and
Power to Prosper Journal* and my *Kept Promises Journal*. These I
modify to become a conversation with God during meditation.

First, I read through my list of Scripture promises (see Resources).
When I feel the Holy Spirit highlighting a promise, I write it down
in the Kept Promises journal. I copy any of the entries that relate

to this promise. These remind me of the ways God has fulfilled that specific promise in my life.

Here is an example: Psalm 34:18 reads, "The Lord is close to the brokenhearted and saves those who are crushed in spirit." I use it this way: "You are close to me when I am brokenhearted, Lord. You save me when I am crushed in spirit." I call this version "reflected [to God] and personalized."

Because it takes a bit of time, I may spread this exercise over several afternoons. Sometimes I do it on my Sabbath—an entire day when I focus on the Lord. My *Promises and Power to Prosper Journal* has been a wonderful encouragement for me. I feel it is well worth the time it takes, and it is a real mood changer!

I also keep a journal I call *Remembering Cheri.* This is a series of articles that each begin with the same phrase. "One thing I always want to remember about Cheri is . . ." Topics for the articles include her courage, her growing-up stories, her devotion to the family, her faith, etc.

I also refer to my *GriefShare* workbook for some particularly good journaling starters. I usually find them at the bottom of the "My Weekly Griefwork" section of each week's chapter.

AFTERNOON RESETS

After work, I take another break. Before I start cooking and cleaning, I spend time being intimate with God. Whenever possible, I go the beach or the forest. Sometimes I pour my heart out to God in prayer. Sometimes I personalize Scripture, inserting my own name, and read it aloud to Him. This feels like I'm reading God's love letters to me back to Him. I've used a little devotional called *Overcoming Tough Times* extensively in this same way. I read it aloud to the Lord as if He's sitting next to me. I have come to know that He actually is! Like quiet times and walkie-talkies, these resets are a regular part of my daily routine.

PRAISE AND MEDITATION BREAKS

When I sense my peace is shrinking during a workday, I take a break from work. I use the break to sing a praise or worship song. Sometimes it takes more than one song to regain my peace.

I often meditate on Scripture while driving, walking/hiking, or at reset time. I begin by emphasizing the first word of each phrase or sentence as I speak it aloud, pausing after the emphasis to allow the Holy Spirit to impress new truth.

For example: "*You* (pause) are close to me when I am brokenhearted, Lord. *You* (pause) save me when I am crushed in spirit." The next time around, I emphasize the next word: "You *are* (pause) close to me when I am brokenhearted, Lord. You *save* (pause) me when I am crushed in spirit." The next time through I emphasize the third word. I continue this process until I have emphasized every word in the passage. I have found this to be an extremely powerful peace-restoring practice. I believe it is also renewing my mind and creating new and healthier neural pathways in my brain and positive feelings in my heart.

Also, I love to fall asleep listening to recordings of Scripture read aloud. I sleep more soundly and get to sleep more quickly when I do this.

Keeping the Sabbath
Cheri and I found a day of rest and worship to be an indispensable exercise as we fought the cancer attack against her. It has become much more important for me since Cheri's passing. I try to follow the Holy Spirit's prompting for activity, which usually looks like extended versions of an assortment of the disciplines detailed here.

Getaways
Just after Cheri passed, I felt I *had* to get away. The evidence of her presence throughout our home was too much for me. Cheri designed and planned our home, picked all the fixtures, finishes, appliances, and systems, and decorated it too. I simply could not bear it for months on end, and it still feels like that at times. But, after over three years, it's more tolerable somehow. I can now go longer between getaways.

I begin to lose focus and perspective if I stay home too long, so in the summer, I go camping. That first year, I went to the mountains every other week for three to five days. The last two years, it's been every third week. My dog Duncan and I hike and climb mountains; small ones—I'm old. I love meditating while we're hiking. I also have favorite "perches" where I can sit before some magnificent scenes of God's handiwork. In the winter, I like to do sleepovers at my kids' places. Sometimes, I visit out-of-town friends and relatives in their homes. These getaways, though still restorative, are no longer as absolutely necessary as they once were.

If some of these ideas appeal to you, try them for yourself. Hopefully, they will lead you to other ideas uniquely your own. Ask the Holy Spirit to inspire you in this way. That is part of His job description, after all. Scripture says He came to "guide us into all truth" John 16:13.

As I have followed these habits throughout my grieving process, I have found deeper peace and intimacy with God—I like to say it "into-me-see"—than ever before. In the darkest days of my life I have found comfort and counsel in ways I never before even imagined. I pray you will too!

DISCUSSION QUESTIONS

1. Have you received Jesus as your Savior? If so, please share that experience with the group. Some know they have done so but do not remember the specific moment when they began their relationship with God. Others experienced a distinct encounter with God when they first trusted Jesus. I (Bruce) first gave my life to Jesus in Sunday school when I was eight and a half. In my late teens I snatched it back in rebellion but gave it back to Him in my early forties, desperate amid the wreckage I had made of my life and family.

   Everyone's moment of introduction to Jesus as Lord and Savior is unique, so we hope you will share your own personal experience with others.

   _____

   _____

   _____

   _____

   _____

   _____

   _____

   _____

   _____

2. If you have not yet received Christ, are you (a) still contemplating the decision, or (b) do you have some questions about receiving Christ, or (c) are you not yet ready? Please describe.

   _____

   _____

   _____

   _____

   _____

_____

_____

_____

3. If you replied to the previous question with answer "a" or "b,"
   your group leader or a pastor will be happy to discuss any
   questions you may have. Write them here for future reference.

_____

_____

_____

_____

_____

_____

_____

_____

_____

4. If you have already received Christ, which of the ideas in this
   chapter do you see yourself using to increase your intimacy
   with Jesus? What ideas of your own do you have? What might
   that look like in your life?

_____

_____

_____

_____

_____

_____

_____

_____

_____

Balance Suffering In Communion and Community

Give your broken heart to God and His people
to receive healing from both.

CHAPTER TWO

Balance Suffering in Communion and Community

BIND UP THE BROKENHEARTED

The Spirit of the Sovereign Lord is on me . . .
He has sent me to bind up the brokenhearted
(Isaiah 61:1).

Pain is inevitable, but misery is optional.
Max Lucado[2]

The surest way to misery I (Bruce) know is to try to carry the loss of Cheri by myself. It's too much for me! To attempt it is to be crushed. I know because I have tried to carry it. Sometimes I still try—always with that same result. It crushes my heart.

Why do we men try to live by the credo, "Big boys don't cry" or, perhaps, "Real men can handle whatever life brings them"? We think it's the independent, "American way," after all. But that's a trap!

SURFING THE WAVES

The grief of losing Cheri has come at me in waves. In the beginning, they were really big waves. I believe the Holy Spirit taught me that getting through it is a lot like surfing. If I choose to, I can ride a wave of grief. I can experience its power and yield to the impulse to use spoken or written words. Sometimes I weep, wail, or howl to fully express the emotion. Once I have done this, the wave dissipates. I land safely on the beach of my day and continue on my way.

When I resist the wave, I get pounded into the beach of my day. I struggle to maintain focus on simple tasks. I am easily irritated and even angry about trivial stuff. I've learned that continually stuffing my feelings can lead to becoming bitter. I can even become stuck right there in my grief.

I have also found that I can delay riding the waves of grief. My

---

2   Worthy Inspired, *Overcoming Tough Times: God's Answer To Every Situation* (New York: Worthy Publishing, 2016), p. 58.

heart seems to accept it if I tell myself, "I want to put away the groceries I just brought home, and *then* I will ride this wave with you." My heart will even accept a calendared appointment for tomorrow. I must keep this appointment, however, because my heart does not like to be ignored!

§

I (Chris) have set appointments to ride the grief wave several times. My problem is actually keeping the appointments. I made an appointment with grief to watch the photo collage shown at my late wife's memorial service. I put sticky notes on my computer monitor to remind me. I would set the notes aside as other things suddenly became more important. I knew that it would be good for me. I needed it. I knew the Lord would bring me through it. But I still hesitated to start the video.

Looking deeper into my heart revealed fear. I was afraid of the emotional pain I would experience. I did not look forward to that part of the process. The wave was not soft or comfortable. It seemed more like the waves in Hawaii shown in the movie *Jaws*, which were in excess of sixty feet. The extent of my emotional pain was exceedingly difficult and could turn me into a blubbering mess in about two minutes. "Don't want to go there," my heart would say.

It is kind of like going to the dentist. No one *likes* to go, but it sure is nice when you walk away at the end; therefore, we go. I watched the video several times. Each time, I would eventually come through to the other side of my grief wave. I would feel great until the next time the video would call me again.

Helpful? Yes. Good for me? Yes. Was Jesus there in the wave? Yes. Was it emotionally painful? Yes, but God used it to move me forward in my journey. I call this type of communion-grieving with Jesus "purposeful grieving." Now I pay attention to the sticky notes.

Another type of communion-grieving I've done is just as purposeful, but lighter. It's having a conversation with Jesus while walking the beach. I like to do it on a nice day. No crashing grief waves here. Rather, it is always a deep, two-way conversation about how things are going. There is also a good mix of lighter emotion. As we walk, we talk. It is a time of sharing my feelings about various aspects of grieving. My walk always ends at a bench where there is a memorial brick implanted in the walkway. I call it my brick, though I do not know its origin. The message on the brick is simple: "Strength for the day. Peace through the night. Joy in our journey." I believe Jesus placed that brick just for me. It is wonderful to commune in that place, as it brings me so much comfort and joy. To this day, ten years later, it is still one of my favorite places. *That's communion in the suffering.*

§

COMMUNION AND COMMUNITY

For me (Bruce), suffering in communion sometimes includes walking and talking with Jesus or riding the grief wave with Him. It always involves directing my outward expressions to God alone. He is always with me, after all. I ask God, "What comfort and counsel do you have for me today?" I like to record any impressions I receive from Him to refer to later. I can forget easily—especially since Cheri passed. I even forget things I thought I'd *never* forget.

These impressions might include, "Reschedule those afternoon appointments." And, "Let's do something mindless—like laundry." And, "You need some 'lap time' with Me. Read Me a story of My love for you from Psalms." These are ways I present my broken heart to the Lord, and He binds up my broken heart.

§

I (Chris) believe it is absolutely necessary to balance grieving in communion and community. Even pastors and other Christian leaders need the comfort that comes from mourning in community. About six months after my wife died, I was asked by my church leadership to help lead a grief class. I guess they thought six months was enough for me! After all, I had years of pastoral and counseling ministry behind me. The first night, I went to class expecting to be the leader, but as people began to share, I realized, "I'm not doing too well here." By the time it was my turn to share my loss, I was in tears. I couldn't be there for the group. I was not ready. I was there for *me*. I needed the support of the group more than anyone else.

This became my first adventure in processing grief. I gained so much from sharing in community with others who understood. I loved on them, and they loved on me. As I made myself vulnerable in this class, I didn't lose one ounce of credibility with church leadership or with others in the congregation. All this was very healing for me.

§

Here's how I (Bruce) define suffering in community. After I have processed my feelings with Jesus, I am able to share with others a more condensed and coherent account of my suffering. I often share with my widowed men's grief group. At times, I share with my men's Bible study partners. Very often it's with one of my "listening friends." These are compassionate male friends who have volunteered to hear stories of my grief journey.

It's important that my "listening friends" be men, because this kind of transparency leads to intimacy. At just over three years into my grief journey, I am not yet ready for a new primary relationship. I know my heart is still damaged, as I'm still too easily irritated. I know I can unintentionally and unwittingly hurt others.

As I have practiced sharing my broken heart with God's people, He has built a genuinely caring community around me. These men have been able to truly see my grief. They have grown in compassion for and connection with me. They really *get* me, and this also binds up my broken heart.

BALANCE
The balance between communion and community is not static. That is, the balance point often changes from day to day. During workdays, my times of solitude tend to be shorter, and I spend a lot of time with others. On my rest days, I find solitude in sharing my heart with Jesus. Sometimes, I ask, "Jesus, what do You have for me today?"

The impression I get is something like, "You've been by yourself too much lately. You need some community. Call Mike today." Or, "You've gone from one meeting to another all week. Take a walk with Me by the lake. Let's talk, just you and Me."

The point is, I can't see myself very well. I really need the Lord's perspective. That requires communion and communication with Him. Very often, I'll hear Jesus ask me, "How's your heart, Bruce?" In sharing the answer with Him, I discover that I'm lacking peace. I realize my balance point needs attention.

I believe God is more interested in the condition of my heart than the number of things I've accomplished today. The Bible backs up this idea: "The Lord does not look at the things people look at. People look at the outward appearance, but the Lord looks at the *heart*" (1 Samuel 16:7b, emphasis added). If you look at my outward appearance, I can fool you. I can *look* like I have it all together. In reality, my heart could be in an uproar of pain. It could be breaking all over again, but I'm just not showing it on the outside.

HEARING FROM GOD

God speaks to us in many ways. He knows how to communicate with each of us personally.

Often, I hear from God through pictures, rather than words. I don't actually hear, "You've gone from one meeting to another all week." Instead, I'll see a series of images flash in my mind. This is followed by the image of me walking at the lake and talking with Jesus.

I've studied the various ways people hear from God. Imagery is common. So is the sense of hearing words spoken. So is seeing them written in the mind. Some people experience a shift in their emotions when God speaks. They may feel peace replacing turmoil, for instance. And finally, some experience a shift in thinking or believing. For example, one may have held a lifelong belief that insisted, "No one cares for me." When God speaks, that belief becomes, "Jesus just can't get enough of me."

DISCUSSION QUESTIONS

1. How do you hear from God? What does that sound/look/feel like for you?

_____

_____

_____

_____

_____

_____

_____

_____

_____

_____

_____

_____

_____

2. What does communion/solitude with God look like for you?

_____

_____

_____

_____

_____

_____

_____

_____

_____

_____

_____

3. Processing my grief well means that I get to tell my story. Who are your listeners? What does the rest of your caring community look like? What would you like to do to expand that community?

_____

_____

_____

_____

_____

_____

_____

_____

_____

_____

_____

_____

4. Sometimes grief can ambush us. These grief attacks can vary in intensity and impact. Have you ever experienced a grief ambush? How did others help you?

_____

_____

_____

_____

_____

_____

_____

_____

_____

_____

_____

5. Shortly after her husband Bob died, the Lord showed Mary Beth Woll this picture of her heart, blown to smithereens by the trauma of her loss.

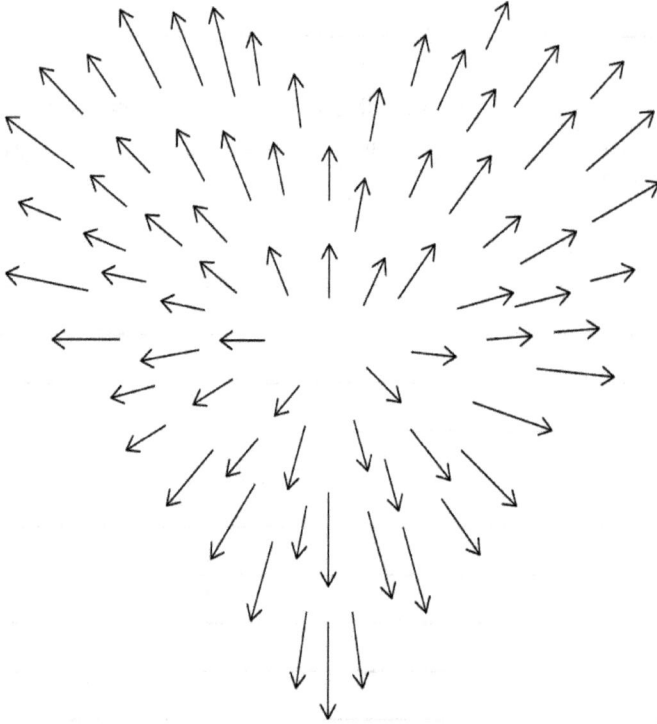

When God healed her broken heart, He gathered up all the fragmented pieces, fit them back together again, and made something new and beautiful.

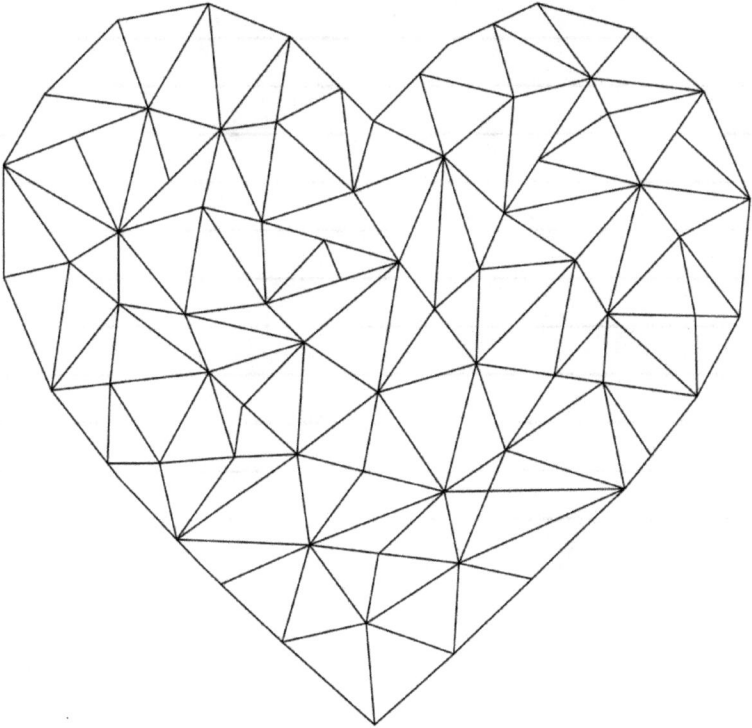

The drawings had such an impact on me that I asked Mary Beth to allow me to share them with you.

6. In what ways have God and His people bound up your broken heart? What would you like to do so that you can experience more of this?

_____

_____

_____

_____

_____

_____

_____

_____

_____

_____

_____

Connection Leads to Freedom

To become truly healed, share your story
with safe significant others as well as with Jesus.

CHAPTER THREE

Connection Leads to Freedom

PROCLAIM FREEDOM FOR THE CAPTIVES

The Spirit of the Sovereign Lord is on me . . .
to proclaim freedom for the captives and release
from darkness for the prisoners (Isaiah 61:1).

When I (Bruce) felt Jesus was saying I was free, it was great news! I truly felt captured by grief in the year after Cheri passed. It was a very dark prison for me. I wasn't a stranger to loss. I had lost my dad, my mom, and a cousin. The cousin was my closest family friend. I also had lost several other close friends. But this, *this* was different! I found myself crying, wailing, and even howling like an animal. I experienced pain as never before in my life. My ability to focus on any but the simplest tasks was non-existent. I've been a lifelong voracious reader. I often read weighty books. Now I found I couldn't make sense of anything but a very short article.

In a class on grief, I learned that failing to process my grief could leave me stuck in that prison for years. The imprisonment could even last the rest of my life. I desperately wanted to be free, so I pressed into that caring community I described. That community functioned as Jesus' Body in just the sense of Isaiah 61:1. Over time, it facilitated my release and escape from that prison.

At this point in my journey, I am a little over three years into it. I still return to gentle weeping at times; however, it's no longer dark there when I do. Instead of lamenting my loss, I can thank God with all my heart for the impact Cheri had, and continues to have, on my life. I thank Him for the wonderful memories I have of life with her. I thank Him for all the joyful ways He used us as a couple. Most often the tears are tears of gratitude, not sorrow. Just now, I can often string together several days without going to the grief prison at all.

SHARE THE STORY

Martha Whitmore Hickman quotes Holocaust survivor Elie Wiesel who said, "Whoever survives a test, whatever it may be, must tell the story. That is his duty."[3] She says it this way: "To tell our story is a way of affirming the life of the one we have lost—the experiences we had together, the favorite family stories. To tell the story is also a way of moving our grief along, and so contributes to our own healing. But it is also a gift to others . . . how we got through it. Our friends will come to their crises of loss soon enough. Perhaps we can ease the way for them."[4]

Yes! This kind of connection *does* lead to freedom. It's really this simple. If I choose to isolate, I risk getting stuck in my grief. I risk becoming angry, bitter, or depressed. I risk being of little use to anyone, including me. If I choose short-term relief, the same thing is likely to happen. This kind of relief can involve busyness or numbing the pain. Some do this with alcohol, drugs, or comfort food. Others numb the pain by casual sex or jumping immediately into a new primary relationship. Shopping is also short-term relief for some; however, short-term relief in whatever form is *avoidance of,* not the *solution for,* grief. As I learned early on in a grief group: "I can't get over it; I can't get around it; I must go *through* it." I must feel the feelings and tell the stories, expressing them outwardly, aloud or in writing. *That* is the road to freedom.

PRIORITIZING GRIEF WORK

I am fortunate in that I am a retired person. When Cheri died, much of my work was volunteer work—work I could withdraw from to free up time to focus on grief work. Also, our children are grown and have families, careers, and homes of their own. I did not have the pressures of a job and raising children. I know not every widowed guy is like that; however, prioritizing grief work *does* bear fruit. This is true no matter what that may look like. It doesn't matter how brief the time spent may be. Doing the work moves folks forward in their grief journey. I have seen it clearly in the lives of other grievers. In my caring community there are those who still have jobs and have children at home. They can devote less time to their grief journey than I can. Still, as they do what they can, they move forward.

3   Martha Whitmore Hickman, Healing After Loss: Daily Meditations for Working Through Grief (New York: Collins, an imprint of HarperCollins Publishers, 1994), p. 30.
    4   Ibid.

BRUCE'S STORY

Cheri discovered she was being attacked by breast cancer in the summer of 2012. Together, we fought the cancer for over five years. On December 14, 2017, it took her life.

Neither of us accepted defeat until the day before Cheri passed. We were in a war. It was often as chaotic as war can be. We believed we could not win this war if we accepted that we could lose. Both of us believed God was leading us. We saw ample evidence surrounding us that it was true. He gave us the courage, persistence, and power to fight that five-year war. We believed all the while that we *would* win.

Cheri did win. She's right where she always wanted to be—face to face with Jesus. And I will win, too. Walking with Jesus, I believe I will walk all the way. I'll come *through* the valley of the shadow of death (Psalm 23:4, NASB). I'll come through the door of grief's prison to freedom.

§

CHRIS'S STORY

I sincerely hope others will be emboldened by my telling my story and *take heart* to share *their* stories. Maybe others will identify with it and begin to feel hope in the midst of sorrow and pain. I hope this. I pray this. I believe this.

My personal journey to freedom by way of connection begins with Irene's illness. We had been pastoring in Weiser, Idaho for a couple of years where the ministry was going well. Without warning, Irene began to have blinding headaches and blurred vision. She could not walk a straight line. We could not keep up with the many things going wrong at the same time.

There were doctor after doctor after doctor visits, but no one had an answer. A couple of the doctors thought she had multiple sclerosis, but Irene's symptoms were not consistent with that disease. Finally, our old family doctor decided to test her for Lyme disease. Bingo! It was 1990 when that diagnosis began a twenty-year journey of ups and downs that included ever-increasing medications, along with mental and emotional devastation. Early on, there were some good seasons when it seemed things were really okay. These times became fewer as time went on and Irene's body began a long slide to no return.

We had left our pastorate in Port Townsend, Washington around 2001 and had extended ourselves into emotional health ministry. God was blessing Candlelight Ministries, the nonprofit we had developed, and we were excited about it.

However, Irene's health kept on its downward swing. To get around, she needed a wheelchair or walker. The twenty-five or so medications she was taking had taken their toll on her body. The last five years were troublesome.

By this time, I was at the end of my strength. I cried out to God, "Why aren't You doing something? What happened to healing? Why are You so silent to my cries?"

The ministry had gone to zero and we were totally isolated. Our house was a nursing home with me as the primary caregiver. When not at work, I was home at work, often all night. Although we still made it to church, it was more of a chore than a blessing. I was feeling done, my life gone, and spent. I felt empty with nothing left to give.

On December 23, 2010, Irene passed away. Asleep by her side, I suddenly awakened at 3 a.m. and knew she was gone. It was as if she woke me up to tell me she was going home. She was finally free. The Lord gave me a picture of her filled with joy in heaven. I, however, was not free or joyful.

Grief was a new thing to me. Oh, I knew the theory; after all, I was a pastor and had done lots of funerals in my day. I knew the stages of grief. I was a seasoned veteran on emotional wellbeing and wholeness. Of course, theory doesn't function like experience does.

I thought I began the grief journey pretty well. I had taken care of the memorial planning and talked to my family. Got through Christmas. Cried when I needed to. I still went to church and met regularly with my Bible study, but in reality, I was a mess.

I had not yet really started on the grief journey. I had not begun to deal with all the stuff on the inside of me. I needed to not only deal with the loss of Irene, but also with the emotional impact of no longer being a long-term primary caregiver. There seemed to be a missing element in this whole process.

THE POWER OF CONNECTION

I was in jail and could not see the bars. I was in a prison of grief and did not know it. I thought it was business as usual for me, but I did not realize I was stuck. *I got this*, I thought. *Not!*

My first experience with connection came with my attendance at a grief processing group. That course revealed my true condition, and I realized I was not making my way out of it.

I've come to find that most life-changes start with a revelation that gives insight on the true state of our being. My experience was just that. But what I needed most was to connect with others to help me walk out this revelation. I also needed the right context for connecting with others. I needed others who were in the middle of their grief as I was.

As classmates told their stories, I gained strength and understanding. I also gained a lot more compassion. I found I desperately needed and wanted to tell my story. It didn't come out all in one sitting. As we did the lessons, I found ample room to get it out and on the table. With a safe group of people, I found telling my story was powerfully comforting and healing. I went home each night feeling a little more down the path than when I came. I am so grateful for that connection. I knew I was not alone, nor did I have to do it alone.

Another kind of connection I experienced was with a retired pastor who stood in the courtyard of the church every Sunday, positioning himself to greet or pray with anyone coming in. Every Sunday, I found myself going up to him. I knew he would ask, "How are you doing, Chris?" He really *did* want to know how I was doing. Even on days when I just wasn't into it, there he'd be, smiling away, as if I were the only one he was there for. I never escaped, and I'm glad I didn't. Our interaction was short, to the point, and gut-level honest. A short prayer, and I was free—until next week. I'll never forget that connection. It was powerful and reassuring, full of grace, and it gave me a few moments to tell my story.

A rather unique connection came when I was invited to speak at a seniors' group, sharing my testimony about my loss. I did tell my story but also added what God was telling and teaching me in the grief process. I knew I was not yet finished with my journey. However, I had many things to share about what God was showing me. Those in the seniors' group who had gone through the process understood my sharing.

Being involved with *what* God is doing is sometimes better than answering all the whys. Often when we tell our story, we reveal the pain involved. We may share our struggle to understand many of the whys and what-fors. There are usually a number of truths that God would have us share. If we have adopted unhealthy mindsets or belief systems, focusing on this *what* can have a marked effect on how we are doing. Here it is truth that really sets us free and moves us forward. Having the right context for this kind of connection can bring enormous healing. It comes when we hear it rehearsed through our own voice.

DISCUSSION QUESTIONS

1. With whom can you or *do* you share your grief story?

   _____

   _____

   _____

   _____

   _____

   _____

   _____

   _____

   _____

   _____

2. As we journey through our grief, we may discover mindsets and thinking patterns that are not helpful. As we apply God's Word to these areas, we will experience growth and freedom. What are some of these areas in your life?

   _____

   _____

   _____

   _____

   _____

   _____

   _____

   _____

   _____

3. If you were free in these areas, how would your life be different? What would that look like?

_____

_____

_____

_____

_____

_____

_____

_____

_____

_____

_____

_____

4. As widowed men, we may need help from others to be set free. In what ways do you see yourself needing others in the process of becoming free? Who could you ask for help in these areas?

_____

_____

_____

_____

_____

_____

_____

_____

_____

_____

_____

_____

5. What truths of God have you discerned through your grief journey? How have they ministered to you? How could you find a place of connection with others for sharing them?

_____

_____

_____

_____

_____

_____

_____

_____

_____

_____

_____

_____

GROWING STRONGER GUIDELINE #4

Throw Off What Hinders

With God's Help, Get Rid of It!

CHAPTER FOUR

Throw Off What Hinders
WITH GOD'S HELP, GET RID OF IT!

*Let us throw off everything that hinders and the sin
that so easily entangles, and let us run with perseverance
the race marked out for us (Hebrews 12:1).*

When you've got a strong enough why, you
can always find the how. Zig Ziglar[5]

This principle is a hard one for me (Bruce). It got hard when Cheri passed. My willpower, or "want-to," as I call it, went to pieces. Along with it went my memory, energy level, and health. There were many days in the beginning when I didn't want to even get out of bed. My reason for doing it just wasn't strong enough to fuel my will. My "why," as Ziglar calls it, was weak. And often I *didn't* get up until much, much later than usual. After I finally left the bed, I had trouble getting motivated. It was hard to even get dressed, much less clean the house. It was hard to take showers or do my prescribed physical therapies. And it just went on and on. I'm sure you get the picture. Maybe you've experienced it yourself.

The name of this race we're running is "The Grief Journey." The "race marked out for us" (Hebrews 12:1) runs from mourning to joy. In the beginning of the race, I couldn't envision myself as joyful. I could not even *imagine* myself crossing that finish line. I was hoping the race was a sprint. Sprinters can see the finish line from the start. I was disappointed to learn that the grief journey is a marathon. It is grueling, demanding, and longer than anyone wants it to be. Nevertheless, I persevered with my grief work over the next three years. That has brought me now to flashes of joy. I can *now* envision myself finishing the race. I can see myself living in the new normal of joy.

WHAT'S HOLDING YOU BACK?
This lack of want-to was not just confined to helpful things. It carried over into things that hindered my grief journey. For example,

5   https://afamuche.com/zig-ziglar-quotes/.

there were friends who suggested I should be "over it" by now. That was decidedly *not* helpful for me to hear. My self-confidence was at an all-time low. So was my confidence in who God made me to be. I questioned the amount of time I was spending on grief work. *That* was certainly a hindrance to doing it!

I stubbornly held on to those relationships as I knew I needed friends. I didn't immediately "throw them off" (Hebrews 12:1). I could have sought more compassionate friends to replace them. Still, I felt the Holy Spirit drawing me to make grief work my highest priority.

The good news is that my want-to is coming back. I have replaced those friendships with new ones. These friends have become part of the caring community I have described. They have actually *accelerated* my healing process.

So, I was dealing with two hindrances. One was the unhealthy friendships themselves. The other was my lack of want-to. I have always been a disciplined person. After all, my middle name is William. I like to say it "Will-I-am." I like habits, and I can stick to them. After Cheri passed, the only habits I seemed to stick to were things that weren't the best for me. In a grief group, I learned that lessening of one's willpower is a common experience among grievers. That helped me persevere in spite of the discouragement I felt at my failures. That knowledge gave me hope that it was a phase that would eventually pass.

Identifying what slows me down is the first step in getting rid of it; however, it was hard for me to see what some of those things were. Some of them were very much a part of my life. I simply could not identify them as hindrances. It was like I was carrying a heavy backpack. It was fixed to me. I could not take it off to see what was inside, so I asked the Lord to look. "Lord, what am I carrying that's slowing me down?" He was faithful to show me as I persisted with the question. The point here is to ask, "What's holding *you* back?" Naming the hindrances is the first step to getting rid of them. Without a target, there's nothing to shoot at.

WITH GOD'S PARTNERSHIP, GET RID OF IT!

The next step toward freedom is a choice. I must choose to get rid of the hindrance. If I don't want it, I won't ask for it. When folks came to Jesus for healing, He often asked them something like this:

"What do you want from Me?"

When the petitioner responded, "I want to see (walk, be free, etc.)," *then* He healed them. The wanting and the asking go together. I asked Jesus for freedom from the hindrances he showed me. And He gave it to me by taking those hindrances right out of my heart.

Now He's using the process of mind renewal. He's creating new and positive neural pathways in my brain that are based on trust in God. These new thought processes replace the old, hindrance-based pathways of thought. He is removing the anxious churning of my mind that used to characterize my life.

In its place, there is peace. I have an improved ability to focus on things at hand. I carry a huge load of gratitude to Jesus for His mercy and healing. That load doesn't hinder—it helps!

If He did it for me, He'll do it for you. You get to start the process: choose and ask. Jesus, speaking to His disciples, once said, "You shall know the truth, and the truth shall make you free . . . Therefore, if the Son makes you free, you shall be free indeed" (John 8:32,36, NKJV).

§

I (Chris) agree that the grief journey can be a long-distance race like a marathon. There's plenty of time for hindrances to sneak in on the process. Some of these hindrances may be entirely based in the grief journey itself. Others come from deep within our past. The grief just brings them to the surface. It doesn't matter whether they're current or past in origin. As Hebrews 12 tells us, they are to be tossed aside so we can better run the race. They need to be processed or dealt with in order to move forward. This is true not only in grief, but also in our life with Jesus. This is especially needed when it is the Holy Spirit that brings them to awareness. I would like to suggest three areas that are of importance in overcoming hindrances.

THE POWER OF CHOICE

This kind of choice is choosing to move forward despite what I feel. I must make up my mind to move. We make choices all the time to help us to face our fears and step through our various misgivings. I guess you could call it courage. As John Wayne said, "Courage is being scared to death . . . saddling up anyway."[6]

I was at Sol Duc Hot Springs on Washington's Olympic Peninsula enjoying the really hot pool. A few feet away was a large swimming pool. Since it was a hot day, I thought about doing a few laps but wondered why there was only one other person there in the pool. When I stuck my foot in to check the temperature, it was ice cold. Swimming laps was suddenly off the menu. I was at the edge, ready to dive in. I could walk away, or I could just go for it. "No guts, no glory," I thought as I dove in. The shock was intense, but I did not freeze to death! Out of the pool and back to the hot tub, I felt invigorated, so I did it several more times. I loved the hot to cold and back again and now enjoy this process every time I go to Sol Duc.

The power of choice got me on the right road in a lot of areas, even my choice to move forward in my grief journey. If you also want to "saddle up," Jesus can also ride along with you. He is a great encourager.

THE POWER OF WILL

"Are you willing?" I've used this phrase hundreds of times as people have shown up in my office full of want-tos and questions. Often there seems to be a missing element. Some just want the hindrances gone. They want God to take away all their pain and their humanness.

I've then asked them, "Are you willing to give it away?"

We must all ask ourselves:

- Am I willing to go to the places that are filled with pain and trauma?
- Can I let Jesus touch them?
- Am I willing to let Jesus show me why this hindrance is there and how it got there in the first place?
- If I am not willing, can I go to Jesus and tell Him why I'm not?

This is partnering with the Lord in this process.

Please remember that while God is absolutely sovereign, He is not a control freak. He will not override your will. He won't force you to do something you do not want to do. That would be counter

6   https://jhumpoo.com/john-wayne-quotes-about-courage/#john-wayne-quotes-on-courage.

to His character. Instead, He will invite you over and over again into His plan for you.

If we are willing to give our pain and trauma to Jesus, we will be positioned for the removal of the hindrances that beset us. The possibilities are endless. The question is, "Am I willing to allow Jesus to speak into my hindrances? Can I accept His strength to throw them off?"

THE POWER OF TRUTH

In John 8:32,36, Jesus said, "Then you will know the truth, and the truth will set you free." Again, He said, "So if the Son sets you free, you will be free indeed." Set free? That sounds good. Indeed. You mean like totally free to the point that I don't have to work on it anymore? Exactly! Some synonyms for "indeed" include: in reality, truly, actually, in truth, to be sure, as a matter of fact.

A belief system can be described as a heart belief or a core belief; truth that is planted firmly with no doubt in my innermost being. At times this goes well beyond my intellect or even my understanding. However, it *does* set me free.

Most of the time, negative feelings are not about my circumstances. They are about what I *believe* about my circumstances. I have accepted a lie that has lodged in my heart, not just in my mind. It makes me feel terrible. It would be nice if we walked out in life all we knew. If we have been Christians a while, we know some Scripture. The problem is we just may not believe all we know. Our core beliefs influence *everything,* so we walk out what we believe more than what we know.

How does this work in ridding the hindrances so we can run the race? Here's a simple equation: Heart beliefs influence emotions, which influence behavior.

Check out the following conversation between Joe and Ed.

"I've been invited to a grief processing group, but I'm not going," says Joe.

"Why not?"

"Hey, I'm a professional and can't let all this stuff show on the outside."

"What would happen if you did, Joe?"

"Are you kidding? There are people who would use it against me. I would have no credibility at all."

"How does that make you feel to believe that?"

"Really bad, terrible, depressed."

"How come, Joe?"

"Because my life would be at an end, and I would have no future at all. I'd be worthless, absolutely worthless."

Now we could try to encourage Joe by quoting Jeremiah 29:11 that talks about having a future and hope. We could encourage him by telling him it's not so. We could gather around and pray. All that is good, and that is what connection is all about. However, it may not bring the desired end. Joe's hindrance is not his refusal to attend the group. It is what he is believing in his heart about going.

If I believed I would end up worthless by going, I wouldn't go either. We respond according to what we believe, even if it is a lie.

Joe really needs to hear the truth from Jesus.

- He must be willing to place his belief and feelings at the feet of Jesus through prayer.
- He must be willing to ask Jesus what the truth is about his circumstances.
- He must be willing to receive God's truth in his heart.

This will change *everything*. Once the lie is replaced with truth, Joe will be ready to go to the grief group.

Of course, this is greatly simplified for clarity, but it works! If I find myself with a hindrance of some kind, I can simply ask, "What am I believing that makes me feel so bad that I will not do _____ and do _____ instead?" Once I find out what I'm believing, I can just take it to Jesus in prayer. He will tell me if it is true or not. If not, He'll tell me His truth concerning the matter. (More on this methodology can be found at *www.transformationprayer.org*.)

In *Don't Lose Heart!*, Mary Beth Woll says, "Deep and permanent change requires more than a decision plus willpower."[7] It requires partnership with God.

---

7   Mary Beth Woll, Linda Smith, and Paul Meier, MD, Don't Lose Heart: A Widow's Guide to Growing Stronger (Everett: The Widows Project, 2020), p. 32.

How do I (Bruce) do that?

- I confide in Him. I name the hindrance, describe my struggle and share how I feel about it all. I "pour out my heart to Him," as Psalm 62:8 suggests.
- I ask for His "comfort and counsel" as I learned in a grief processing group.
- I record my impressions for later reference. Poor recall is another common result of grief. That is slowly improving as I do my grief work.
- I get a lot of support. I lean heavily on my caring community. These are my friends, especially those who have been widowed. My small groups are my grief groups, my men's Bible study, and my coworkers in The Widows Project. In short, I lean heavily on those expressions of Jesus' body that feed my want-to.

God does for us what we can't do for ourselves. I love this encouragement from *Don't Lose Heart!*:

> White-knuckling it may work for a while, but deep and permanent change requires more than a decision plus willpower. To change directions in life, we need clear guidance and lots of support. GriefShare and other widows' groups often provide important comfort, camaraderie, encouragement, and structure. In order to benefit from this support system, it is imperative to stay connected to God and other Christians. Isolation can be risky! Attend church. Join a Bible study. Be sure to surround yourself with those who understand the importance of living a life of godly choices and discarding destructive behaviors.[8]

There it is again. God accomplishes this miracle through a balance of communing with Him and staying connected to Jesus' Body here on earth. It's the soil in which the seeds of life-change grow—"So that you may be mature and complete, not lacking anything" (James 1:4b).

STAY THE COURSE
The first part of that last verse is, "Let perseverance finish its work." Another choice. If I choose to do that, I will put energy and

---

8   Ibid.

time into that perseverance. I will stay on the racecourse to the finish, even if I fall.

My Scottish clan's motto is "hold fast." That motto was engrained in me. Sometimes, I go whining to God about how hard this life-change thing is. Usually, the impression I receive is, "Stay the course, Bruce." It resonates deeply with "hold fast." And *that* gives me the courage and the strength to do it. I can take another positive step and go forward one more day. I once sent a greeting card that said, "Courage is not the absence of fear. It's going ahead anyway." With my Good Shepherd leading, that's what I can do. I can go ahead even when it's hard.

GET UP, AGAIN!

When I was running in competition, I was sometimes afraid to start a race. I was afraid I would fail to finish. Taking that first step required throwing off the fear of failure. Throwing off something involves a decision first. "I want to get rid of this thing." Throwing is the focused, forceful action that baseball pitchers and football quarterbacks use. I threw off my fear of failure by first realizing that I may *not* finish! I realize that people *do* fail. There's no guilt in failing. Not starting at all is a different story, and so is not getting up and back in the race if I fall. That's why I so need Jesus! He alone can forgive my failures. He alone can strengthen my inner self to persevere. He, "The God who started this great work in me will keep at it and bring it to a flourishing finish" (Philippians 1: 6, MSG).

An inescapable fact for me is that I am human. As a human, I *will* fail sometimes. However, 1 John 1:9 (MSG) states, "If we admit our sins—make a clean break from them—He won't let us down; He'll be true to Himself. He'll forgive our sins and purge us of all wrongdoing."

After the confession, I can "Come freely and boldly to where love is enthroned, to receive mercy's kiss and discover the grace we urgently need to strengthen us in our time of weakness" (Hebrews 4:16, TPT). My best understanding of grace is "God's power to become what I am not yet." It is by *that* power that I can get up again and move forward. It is power in this case to do what I haven't yet done. You can too!

DISCUSSION QUESTIONS

1. How would you describe the race you are running? Is it a marathon or a sprint? Why?

_____

_____

_____

_____

_____

_____

_____

_____

_____

2. Ask God to show you how He sees your race. Ask if He sees anything that is slowing you down from running the way you would like. Note it here. Also, note what would be involved in throwing off that hindrance in your life.

_____

_____

_____

_____

_____

_____

_____

_____

_____

3. What are you doing to build your caring community or support system?

_____

_____

_____

_____

_____

_____

_____

_____

_____

_____

4. Remember that we do not run alone or in our own strength. Commit your race to God and ask Him to free you from anything that is slowing you down or causing you to stumble.

_____

_____

_____

_____

_____

_____

_____

_____

_____

_____

_____

Keep Looking Up

Make personal growth an even higher priority
than resolving your grief.

CHAPTER FIVE

Keep Looking Up

STAYING OURSELVES ON JESUS

*God's peace shall be yours, that tranquil state of a soul
assured of its salvation through Christ, and so fearing
nothing from God and being content with its earthly lot
of whatever sort that is, [that peace] which transcends all
understanding shall garrison and mount guard over your
hearts and minds in Christ Jesus (Philippians 4:7, AMPC).*

*You will guard him and keep him in perfect and constant
peace whose mind [both its inclination and its character] is
stayed on You, because he commits himself to You, leans on
You, and hopes confidently in You (Isaiah 26:3, AMPC).*

Just after Cheri passed, my (Bruce's) inner life was anything
but peaceful. Turmoil and panic more accurately describes it.
Only when I focused on God did peace return. The more I focused
on Him, the more that peace grew. And, that peace really *did*
"transcend all understanding" (Philippians 4:7, AMPC). At least it
sure transcended all *my* understanding. The only thing I was doing
differently was "staying my mind" on the Lord (Isaiah 26:3, AMPC).

A friend explained the nautical term for me. He told me that
on sailing vessels, a "stay" is a piece of rigging of a fixed length.
Stays are used to hold the masts firmly in place. Stays cannot be
removed, lengthened or shortened. *Stayed* is how fixed I want my
gaze on Jesus to be.

FOCUS, FOCUS

In the beginning of this journey through grief, my ability to
focus was extremely limited. My attention span could sometimes
be measured in minutes at best! Meditating on Isaiah 30:15 (NLT),
really helped me. It reads, "This is what the Sovereign Lord, the
Holy One of Israel, says: 'Only in returning to Me and resting in Me
will you be saved. In quietness and confidence is your strength.'"

I thought of this returning as "re-turning" or "turning again."

When I realized my focus had drifted, I would simply turn back to Jesus. I usually shifted focus back to Him through one of the disciplines I outlined in Chapter 1.

Have you too experienced forgetting more easily since your wife passed? If so, I want to encourage you. First, be assured that it's considered a normal reaction to loss. And best of all, it gets better with time and effort. That has been my experience as I can now focus on tasks almost as well as ever.

§

I (Chris) recall a story in Mark Chapter 5 when the disciples had taken Jesus in the boat with them. "Let us cross over to the other side," He said, and they did what He told them to do. These were seasoned seamen in the Sea of Galilee, fishermen whose families had fished those waters for generations. They knew everything about it. That was a simple command to obey. What could go wrong?

Then came a storm so fierce that these veteran fishermen were completely disoriented and terrified and believed they were all going to die. Jesus was asleep and His directive to go to the other side was not so easy to believe. They had lost focus and forgot what He told them.

We've all had our share of trials, tough times, mountaintops, and valleys. If we're believers, Jesus has brought us *through* every time, and each time our faith has grown.

But this grief thing is no *ordinary* storm. It can disorient us and fill us with fear. It can challenge the faith of the most decorated veteran of life with Jesus. Suddenly we are not so sure we will make it to the other side. In fact, we may not even be able to see the other side.

These are attacks from the enemy to disrupt our minds and try to disrupt our faith. The truth is, there is an "other side" to our grief. Jesus has already planned for us to make it there. We can arrive there with greater faith than ever.

You might ask, "Okay, so what does that look like?"

I really like this little nugget of practical truth from Hebrews 12:2 (NASB). "Looking only at Jesus, the originator and perfecter of the faith." As I meditate on how this fits with my grief journey, the "looking" turns into a multifaceted gem. Let me tell you another story to illustrate.

A few years ago, I married my wife Carmen. She once went white-water rafting. After putting on helmets, wetsuits, and lifejackets, the group she was with took up their paddles and boarded the raft. Their qualified and experienced guide had probably been down that river 500 times and knew what to do and when to do it. He said, "Keep your eyes on me and do exactly what I tell you and we will have no trouble at all getting through the rapids."

As they approached the first rapid, the guide instructed them, "Left side paddles in; go deep!" Then they plunged into the first fall. Up and down they went, sideways and straight. Sometimes they barely missed boulders on the right and logs on the left.

"Keep your eyes on me and not on the water," their guide said. "Now, right side down, left side up, go deep! You will be just fine. Enjoy the ride."

They all screamed and paddled for dear life, but they all survived. They made it through and entered a calm, easy-flowing part of the river. Paddling together they moved the raft forward, smiling and joking.

After a few moments, their guide called out again, "There's a more difficult section up ahead. Just remember, keep your eyes on me, and do what I tell you. Do that and we'll all be just fine."

And they were just fine. Calm waters soon again surrounded them. Something was different, as the paddlers had come to trust their guide even more. They knew he really knew what he was doing. Everything he told them was true. It didn't matter how many rapids there were on the journey. They had overcome their terror of the river by learning to keep their eyes on the guide and doing exactly what he said.

Their fears were resolved, and their faith had increased. The rafters were all in it together and all grew together through that experience of real community. They had become a team with a common goal and had made it to the end of their journey.

On this grief journey, we can't control the reoccurring waves of grief. The emotional pain that visits again and again will come. When it does, we can roll with it. When the ride through the rapids is over, we can come again to the place of peace and calm.

Just keep looking to Jesus as our Guide. Do what He says in the rapids of grief. He really knows what He's doing. He is a Man of Sorrows and acquainted with grief. He knows every boulder, log, and rapid along the way, and He is really good at bringing us to the other side. We will be just fine. Our fears will be reduced. Our faith will be increased. And we will have taken another step forward in faith. We will move toward maturity, even in the midst of our pain.

§

A Farsighted Perspective

In the first months of my (Bruce's) ride in the rapids of grief, my immediate troubles were intense. I just couldn't focus for very long on anything else. Now, from my vantage point four years later, that's changing. My ability to focus on complex tasks and future possibilities has improved dramatically. That's one of the things that helps me believe I can assist you through the rapids. I'm not suggesting a timeline for you. Rather, I'm encouraging you in doing your grief work. It doesn't matter what that looks like for you. Sticking to it over time will eventually bear fruit—and good fruit at that!

From Crisis to Opportunity

I have found great comfort in Romans 8:28 (AMPC):

We are assured and know that [God being a partner in their labor] all things work together and are [fitting into a plan] for good to and for those who love God and are called according to [His] design and purpose.

What that means to me is that in order for me to find that good stuff, I must love God. That means I'll answer "Yes" when I hear a calling into His design and purpose.

This wasn't about my getting Him to serve my design and purpose—to get through this awful valley immediately—it was about His design and purpose—always that I become more like Jesus. It takes significant time for Him to accomplish that in me.

Once again, I can testify to holding fast to the course. That's doing the grief work He assigns to me. It is transforming me in just that way. I'm more like Jesus than ever. I wish I could show you before and after pictures of my compassion for others. You'd see growth. I'd also show you growth in my ability to listen to their stories. You'd see more growth in what I call my peace quotient (PQ). I believe the differences you'd see between then and now would be dramatic.

FREEDOM FROM FOCUSING ON FEAR

In the first year or so following Cheri's death, I was beset by fear in a variety of ways. Occasionally, those fear episodes came when I was sleeping. The fears were nameless, but intense enough to paralyze me. I couldn't move, couldn't speak, couldn't think of anything but the fear. Sometimes, it seemed the whole night was a nightmare. In the morning, I got out of bed exhausted. Maybe you've felt it too. In addition, I seemed to carry a heavy anxiety in my gut on most days. It was extremely debilitating. It often caused me to do or say things I would not have otherwise done or said. It interfered with my ability to get things done. I would anxiously run from this task to that, finishing nothing. In a grief group, I learned that all of this is common among the bereaved.

The only things that seemed to help were things that focused my mind on Jesus. After all, He had promised me peace. I used rote prayers during my morning walkie-talkies. (I've included a couple in the Resources section at the back of this book.) I meditated on Scripture. I memorized a personal version of Psalm 62:8 (NLT). "I trust You at all times. I pour out my heart to You. You are my refuge, God." When the fears came at night, though I could not speak, I meditated on this in my heart. Usually, somewhere in the middle of the meditation, I'd pour out my fear to Jesus right there. Then, I'd go back to the meditation. Often I'd drift off to sleep before finishing. And I slept soundly! I took praise breaks and short walkie-talkies in the middle of the day. I did this when I recognized anxiety increasing. And . . . God showed up! Over time, the nighttime fear episodes ceased. The daily anxiety was replaced by peaceful and purposeful life.

DISTRACTED BY "THE GOOD"

Earlier in my journey, I got distracted by tasks that needed doing. This was "good" stuff like cooking, housework, shopping, and gardening. I was like Martha in the story in Luke 10:38–42. I became "worried and upset by many things." The tasks I felt I "just *had* to do" took control of me. It took many months for me to recognize when my inner peace had fled. It took even longer before I returned to sit at Jesus' feet, like Mary in Luke's story. The point is, sitting with Jesus *did* work for me. He brought me peace. I believe sitting with Him will work for you too!

STAY ALERT

There really *is* a kingdom of darkness. Satan really *does* want to "steal [from] and kill and destroy" me (John 10:10). The adversary really *does* "prowl around like a roaring lion." He really *is* "looking for someone to devour" (1 Peter 5:8, NLT). He especially hates Jesus-lovers. Our world really *is* a world at war. Some of the "flaming arrows" of Ephesians 6 are his accusations. "You failed in caring for Cheri, Bruce. You should have done more." Even, "It's your fault she died." When I agree with those thoughts, I leave the Kingdom of God and enter the kingdom of darkness.

The good news is this: if I "resist the devil [stand firm against him], he will flee from me" (James 5:7, AMPC). How do I resist him? First, I deny the accusation. After all, it's a lie from the father of them. Then, I state the truth of what Jesus says about me. A counselor has helped me identify some of the deeper-seated lies. Eventually, I have been able to speak aloud the Holy Spirit's impressions to me.

"That's a lie. I did the best I could for Cheri at the time. Jesus impresses me that He is proud of me. He's proud of the way I fought for her life."

When I do this, guess what? The attack goes away! It lifts off my heart and mind and leaves me alone!

In addition to this, there's my physical self. This is my "flesh" as some Bible versions call it. That part of me gets tired. It gets worn out with the rigors of grief. It gets exhausted trying to do alone all the work that Cheri and I used to do. When that happens, that part of me can start begging for relief and comfort. What it says it wants isn't generally the best thing for me. Thankfully, God's grace and His Spirit are available. They strengthen me and enable me to do what I can't by myself. I resist the flesh's begging and turn to God. I allow Him to lead me out of that fleshy trap.

A UNITED FOCUS

Humans were designed to live best in community. Doing so strengthens us. Mary Beth Woll and Linda Smith point this out in *Don't Lose Heart!:* "Scripture says, 'Let US fix OUR eyes' (Hebrews 12:2, emphasis added)." It works best if it's a caring community, as we've discussed previously. These are folks who understand me because we've experienced the same thing. They know Jesus' love, married life, and being widowed—you get the idea.

DISCUSSION QUESTIONS

1. The Lord's Prayer begins with, "Our Father, which art in heaven, hallowed be Thy name" (Matthew 6:9, KJV). Jesus was teaching us to get our eyes on God and His character before we tell Him about our prayer needs. Take a few moments and list some of the ways we can "hallow His name"—bring praise and glory to His name.

    _____

    _____

    _____

    _____

    _____

    _____

    _____

    _____

    _____

    _____

    _____

    _____

    _____

    _____

    _____

2. Read the account of Peter walking on the water in Matthew 14:22–33. What caused Peter to walk on the water? What caused Peter to be afraid? What happened when he was afraid? How does this apply to your grief journey?

_____

_____

_____

_____

_____

_____

_____

_____

_____

_____

3. Taking our eyes off Jesus and looking at the storm around us can cause us to falter in our faith. Focusing on Jesus strengthens our faith, as He is the Author and Perfecter of our faith. What situations in your grief journey have caused you to look at the storm instead of Jesus? List them here, take a moment to praise the Lord for His wonderful presence, and then release those cares to Him.

_____

_____

_____

_____

_____

_____

_____

_____

_____

4. In what ways have you grown stronger than you were before as a result of working through grief?

_____

_____

_____

_____

_____

_____

_____

_____

_____

_____

_____

_____

GROWING STRONGER GUIDELINE #6

Stand Strong

Whenever you feel like giving up, endure.

CHAPTER SIX

Stand Strong

FOR THE JOY SET BEFORE YOU . . . ENDURE!

Finally, be strong in the Lord and in His mighty power. Put on the full armor of God, so that you can take your stand against the devil's schemes . . . so that when the day of evil comes, you may be able to stand your ground, and after you have done everything, to stand. Stand firm then . . . (Ephesians 6:10–11,13–14a).

Be alert and of sober mind. Your enemy the devil prowls around like a roaring lion, looking for someone to devour (1 Peter 5:8).

Those are sobering words! Why does the Bible tell us *four times* in those verses to stand? For one thing, God knows we can easily get caught up in the visible world. We can lose sight of the fact that there is an unseen enemy. We can forget that he is bent on devouring us.

So how can we endure? How can we stand strong? Consider this:

Looking unto Jesus, the Author and Finisher of our faith, who for the joy that was set before Him endured the cross, scorning the shame, and is set down at the right hand of the throne of God (Hebrews 12:2, KJV).

Here's why we spent so much time on tools for grievers in the first few chapters. Those tools are specific ways of "looking unto Jesus" that have worked for me. They've worked for other men as well.

THE ELEPHANT IN THE ROOM

I think it's time we dealt with . . . the elephant in the room. At least, it was a huge elephant in *my* (Bruce's) room. And it seemed to me most everyone tried to ignore it in church or grief classes. I know it's a big deal for most of us guys. We need answers, so here we go.

Cheri and I shared and enjoyed every aspect of each other. We enjoyed sharing our souls—our thoughts, desires, and emotions. We enjoyed sharing what God was doing in us spiritually. In processing all that with the Lord, I have come to see how it is all still active within me. In that very really sense, Cheri lives on in my life. We also enjoyed sharing our physical selves.

Oh, how I miss the feel of her hand stealing into mine! When that physical sharing was gone, it left a big void in my life. The loss of our physical intimacy is still something I'm processing with Jesus. This physical aspect looms large for me.

Therefore, it's an area the enemy of my life attacks regularly. He has the ability to cast thought darts into my mind. They come to me in the first person singular. Thought darts are those "flaming arrows" from Ephesians 6.

Here's how it can look: "Wow, I think this woman likes me. I wonder what being in a relationship with her would be like." He whispers it in just those sorts of words. Then my enemy steps back and waits. He's waiting for me to agree with his thought by taking action. If I do, I'm done—or perhaps better said, *un*done.

This is still difficult, painful, and unresolved for me. So, I'll defer to Chris for insight on this one. He has the perspective of much more time on the grief journey than I.

§

SETTING PARAMETERS IN SEXUALITY

Everyone knows dealing with this reality is difficult in today's moral economy. I (Chris) am offering a brief study which does not answer all questions or address all situations. I want to help you set parameters that will help you live for Jesus as you work out your sexuality. You can manage its expression in real life. What we learned in churches or religious institutions may not be all that helpful; it may not even be accurate or pragmatic. So, let's deal with Scripture and its principles, and maybe we'll come up with a few answers.

In some cases, Scripture, which is our guide for all faith and practice, is very explicit in dealing with sexuality, including: adultery, incest, bestiality, homosexuality, sexual practice within religious rite or practice, fornication or secural practices outside of marriage.

Chapters 18–20 of Leviticus reflect on these practices and the vocabulary used is of special note. For example, Leviticus 20:12 tells us, "If a man lies with his daughter-in-law, both of them shall surely be put to death. They have committed perversion. Their blood shall be upon them." The word perversion is translated in the King James Version as "confusion." It comes from the Hebrew *tebel,* meaning mixture or unnatural.

Other terms are used in these Leviticus portions.

- "Abomination" comes from the Hebrew *tachton*, meaning literally "the bottommost."
- "Wickedness" is from the Hebrew *zammah*, meaning "to have a plan, a bad one, a heinous crime with purpose and with a connotation of lewdness."[9]
- Leviticus 18:6 and following verses uses the term "to look on or uncover the nakedness of others" (KJV). This expression always has a perverse sexual connotation, including homosexuality.

All of these tend to refer to defilement. The Hebrew *tame* means to be "utterly foul, unclean, polluted." In other words, your soul (mind, will, and emotions) is in a separated state. Note: when it includes action, it also includes your body (see 1 Corinthians 6:15–19).

The warning here is clear, especially with the word "confusion." The danger is the breakdown of God-placed natural barriers in the mind.

For example, viewing pornography or participating in such activities breaks down the barriers of right and wrong. Discernment between natural and unnatural fades. The end product is a blurred reality. That opens doors to the acceptance of all these actions as the new norm.

This is very dangerous! Some have said, "I never knew just how bad it could get." Or, "I never intended to view or do such things." Please note: if you are caught in any of these, it would be of great benefit for you to deal with it. The way to deal with it is with the Lord Jesus. It may be good to seek a qualified counselor or minister

---

9   *Strong's Exhaustive Concordance of the Bible with Greek and Hebrew Dictionaries.* Crusade Bible Publishers, Inc. Nashville Tennessee – all defined Hebrew words in this section

to help. Remember, with Jesus, there is always hope.

Now, if you're not in that place, well, good! But you are still a person who is sexually oriented. God made us that way, by the way. How then do we deal with our very real sexuality?

The New Testament often has a sense of "grayness" in this area. It is even silent when it comes to specifics in some cases. It would be nice if it addressed everything, but it just does not. For example, what about making out? How far is too far? What about masturbating, or fantasizing, or just looking? What do I do when remarriage is not on the horizon?

These are great questions, and I must say, difficult to answer. Here are some guidelines we may want to consider when dealing with or expressing our sexuality.

1. DO I FIND MYSELF JUSTIFYING MY POSITION OR ACTION EITHER TO MYSELF OR OTHERS?

You must be very honest with yourself and the Lord. A self-justifying attitude indicates that I am not at peace concerning my actions with the Lord or myself. 1 Corinthians 10:23–24 (NKJV) tells us, "All things are lawful for me but not all things are helpful, all things are lawful for me but not all things edify. Let no one seek his own, but each one the other's well-being." If I satisfy my own lustful cravings with another person by violating Scripture, I am definitely not seeking that other's well-being. 1 Corinthians 6:12 (NKJV) says it this way: "All things are lawful for me, but all things are not helpful. All things are lawful for me, but I will not be brought under the power of any."

Let's examine some of the words in this passage of Scripture:

- **Lawful**: They don't go against Mosaic law but do show the freedom in Christ that exceeds the moral code of Moses.
- **Edify**: AMPC translates it as, "expedient, profitable and wholesome." Helpful for self or others.
- **Not to be brought under the power of any**: Power, from the Greek "exousia" means "to have authority or control over." This is when my freedom has led me to bondage. I am under the control of something else.

2. IS IT DISHONORING TOWARD ANOTHER?

Is my action honoring or dishonoring toward myself or another? Do I care for—love—this person enough not to dishonor them? This will reveal my focus as either self-motivated or other-motivated (see Romans 12:10).

3. IS IT CAUSING ANOTHER TO STUMBLE?

This phrase is often defined as, "to offend, or to make an offense, or placing a rock in front of someone to trip on." To cause another to stumble is to cause another to violate her standards or conscience through my freedom. Therefore, it causes her to sin. In such cases, *I* am the one sinning. Romans 14:21 (NKJV) says, "It is good neither to eat meat nor to drink wine nor do anything by which your brother stumbles or is offended or is made weak." Or, as 1 Corinthians 8:9 (NKJV) reads, "But beware lest somehow this liberty of yours becomes a stumbling block to those who are weak."

4. IS IT JUST AN OCCASION FOR THE FLESH?

Galatians 5:13 (NKJV) says, "For you brethren have been called to liberty, only do not use liberty as an opportunity for the flesh, but through love serve one another." Using my liberty in this way is setting the stage for my own flesh to rise up. I cause *myself* to stumble in my relationship with Christ. When I do this, I am basically violating my own conscience. To do that, I have to set Jesus on the shelf and look the other way. I do this in my mind in order to proceed with getting my flesh what it wants. There's a little self-justification here also. This does not lead to peace.

5. HAVE I CROSSED THE LINE FROM AN EXPRESSION OF SEXUALITY INTO LEWDNESS?

Lewdness is an Old Testament concept. The word is translated from the Hebrew *zammah* and means "to have a plan, a bad one, a heinous crime with purpose and with a connotation of immorality." It has largely to do with where I place my mind, which is extremely important when dealing with these issues. See Romans 7, Galatians 5:17, and Galatians 6:8.

1 Thessalonians 4:3–4 (NKJV) says:

> For this is the will of God, your sanctification, that you should abstain from sexual immorality. That each of you should know how to possess his own vessel in sanctification and honor.

There are a couple of things with which to be challenged here. The first part of that verse says I should know how to possess my own vessel and suggests a very deep relationship with Jesus. That means I am listening to Him in all sincerity as I do this journey with Him in mind. We can possess our own vessels in perfect peace with Jesus. Sanctification means that someone or something is set apart for special service to the Lord. Can I be sanctified and still deal with my own sexuality? Yes! Everyone must set their parameters before the lordship of Christ and do what He says about it.

Masturbation is often a difficult topic. That's because Scripture is silent on the subject. Since Scripture doesn't address this explicitly, then we have to figure it out before the Lord. What other principles does the Bible bring to bear? I have to ask this question: "Is this a viable option as an expression of sexuality for me?" Obviously, only Jesus and I can answer that for myself. "All things are lawful for me, but not all things are helpful" (1 Corinthians 10:23-24, NKJV). There are some things to remember in choosing this option. I must observe the principles listed above.

- I must not move into self-justification.
- I cannot violate my own conscience. Why? Because Jesus has called me to peace.
- As I talk to Jesus about this, He will reveal my personal parameters to me. What may be okay for someone else may not be okay for me. I am not the judge of others who have also worked out their parameters in this gray area.
- I can walk in obedience to Christ and His plan for me as an individual.
- I can walk by faith in this matter. Faith leads to freedom, and freedom leads to peace (Romans 14:22–23).

These guidelines are not exhaustive, nor are they perfect. Prayerfully consider them on your journey with Christ.

§

ANOTHER "WHY"

Because God says so is a *very* big "why." Chris points this out so well. I (Bruce) have another big "why."

When I feel lonely and begin to think about remarriage, I remember what Cheri once told me. She was the love of my life and my best friend ever. She married me within a year of being widowed herself. Some years into our marriage, we began to struggle mightily. Cheri told me she wished we had waited at least a couple of more years. She admitted she really wasn't ready when we married. She hadn't adequately processed her loss. The pain of dealing with her unreadiness complicated things. My hard-heartedness made it even worse. It was very tough for us to deal with our marital struggles. The "dealing with it" took years. We stayed with it and did deal with it. The Lord was faithful to us. He brought us into the wonderful marriage that we eventually enjoyed. I know I'm not alone in this story. I have heard the same thing repeatedly from others who remarried soon after being widowed.

Sometimes, my loneliness starts asking, "Why not start dating again?" Because of my experience, I can say, "I'm not ready. I know I'm not." I *do* know I want desperately to avoid re-experiencing the pain of marrying too soon. That is another big "why" for me. Maybe it can be for you, too.

Zig Ziglar said, "When you've got a strong enough 'why,' you can always find the 'how.'"[10] Avoiding pain and honoring God are my "why." My "how" is to wait to date.

---

10   https://afamuche.com/zig-ziglar-quotes/.

DISCUSSION QUESTIONS

1. After your wife passed, did you experience anything like Bruce's inability to maintain focus? Did you also get caught up in something else? How did it affect your life? How did/will you deal with it?

   _____

   _____

   _____

   _____

   _____

   _____

   _____

   _____

   _____

   _____

   _____

2. Have you experienced attacks from the kingdom of darkness as Bruce described? How did/will you deal with them?

   _____

   _____

   _____

   _____

   _____

   _____

   _____

   _____

   _____

   _____

3. How did your heart react to Chris' explanation of sexual purity as found in Scripture? What do you want to do about it? What is God's best for you?

_____

_____

_____

_____

_____

_____

_____

_____

_____

_____

_____

4. Which of Chris' other points on setting parameters was most impactful for you? What will you do with that going forward?

_____

_____

_____

_____

_____

_____

_____

_____

_____

_____

_____

5. In order to maintain sexual purity, Bruce avoids being alone with one woman in a home or a car. Because he believes prayer is the most intimate thing he can do with another person, he also avoids praying with just one woman, even on the phone. What can you do to work with God to maintain sexual purity?

Take Heart!

When you experience correction, remind yourself
that God is a good Father. Say out loud, "My Daddy
(or Abba, Father or your favorite name for Him) loves me."

CHAPTER SEVEN

Take Heart!

ACCEPT THE LORD'S TRAINING

*God is educating you; that's why you must never drop out.
He's treating you as dear children. This trouble you're in
isn't punishment; it's training, the normal experience of
children. Only irresponsible parents leave children to fend
for themselves. Would you prefer an irresponsible God?
We respect our own parents for training and not spoiling
us, so why not embrace God's training so we can truly live?
While we were children, our parents did what seemed best
to them. But God is doing what is best for us, training us
to live God's holy best. At the time, discipline isn't much
fun. It always feels like it's going against the grain. Later,
of course, it pays off big-time, for it's the well-trained who
find themselves mature in their relationship with God
(Hebrews 12:5–11, MSG).*

I (Bruce) love this particular version of this piece of Scripture. Other versions use the word discipline. They fail to make the connection with *training*. When my dad used to discipline me, it generally hurt! Sometimes it was physical pain, as in "belt discipline." Sometimes it was emotional pain, as in being grounded. Especially in my teens, it hurt to be unable to see my friends. Sometimes, it was hurtful to my self-image. This happened when Dad belittled me for the poor choice I had made. The correction I experienced was motivated by fear. I didn't ever want to experience that pain again. And, brothers, that is not at all like the God I serve! My God is a trainer. He's been showing me His ways to do my life. It started the day I invited Him into it.

GOD IS A GOOD FATHER!

Romans 8:17 says I am a co-heir with Christ. That makes me a son of God! I love how clearly and simply 1 John 3:1a (NLT) puts it. "See how very much our Father loves us, for He calls us His children, and that is what we are!" When He corrects me, it is in love for me. As the opening passage points out, it is for my benefit. At the time of correction, I too often find the discipline isn't much fun. Why?

Because God wants to hurt me? Does He want me afraid to do that again? No! I must admit, it's not fun because change is hard for me; therefore, I don't like it.

Here's an interesting thing I've learned from studying and working with men; we are creatures of habit. The keys go here. These keys are on this hook. Those keys are on that hook. I always know where the keys are. I don't have to spend time looking for them. I can focus on something more important. Dirty laundry goes there. I eat this for breakfast daily at this time. And on and on it goes. One of my mentors says habits enable men to focus very sharply. She says men tend to be single-focused. Meanwhile, women are multi-taskers by nature. Men run DOS, women run Windows.

Another couples' study says it this way: The way the opposite sex operates is "not wrong, just *different*."[11] I have found I am not unique in this. Change is hard for many men.

TAKE HEART!

Another way to say this is "take courage." A follower of Jesus might say, "Humble yourself under His mighty hand." Our opening Scripture says, "Never drop out" on what God is doing to correct you. It says He has a purpose in correcting you. That purpose is for you to mature in your relationship with God. Isn't that the thing we Jesus-lovers want most of all? Ecclesiastes 7:8 (NCV) says it like this: "It is better to finish something than to start it. It is better to be patient than to be proud." I love how Barbara Johnson illustrates this: "If things are tough, remember that every flower that ever bloomed had to go through a whole lot of dirt to get there."[12]

COURSE CORRECTION

One of my first course corrections happened early in my grief journey. It was an impression to make grief work my highest priority. My success would be measured by how much time and effort I gave it. I had all kinds of reasons why this was a bad idea. They were reasons why I didn't need to change. I didn't *want* to change what I was doing. On the other hand, I was talking with God. I was trying

---

11   Integrity Publishers, *Love and Respect: The Love She Most Desires; The Respect He Desperately Needs* (Nashville, TN: Integrity Publishers 2004), term used often throughout.

12   Worthy Inspired, *Overcoming Tough Times: God's Answer To Every Situation* (New York: Worthy Publishing, 2016), p. 16.

to listen and obey, and I just kept feeling that impression. Here's a sample of some of those conversations.

"I don't have time for grief work right now, God. The floors are dirty. I've gotta do some cleaning."

"You will not die if the house is dirty, Bruce. If you don't deal with your loss, you *may* die. You remember what happens when you stuff negative feelings? They have a way of poisoning the body. That can cause it to get sick, right? Why not hire a house cleaner to help you?"

I did, and I started digging deeper into my grief processing workbook.

"I don't have time for my *Remembering Cheri* journal right now, God. The garden is overgrown with weeds. They're spreading. I've gotta get some weeding done."

"You will not die if the garden is overgrown with weeds, Bruce. Is this really about weeds? Isn't it about how you look to others? Please remember that unshed tears contain toxins. These are stored in the body. They poison it, often leading to disease. Do you want to get sick? Why not hire a landscaper to help you?"

I did, and I began working on *Remembering Cheri.*

"I don't have time for a reset this afternoon, God. I'm out of food. I've gotta go shopping."

"You will not die if you don't go shopping right now, Bruce. Your peace for today *may* die if you don't do your reset. Why not go and check the freezer? See what's there. Remember, you froze a bunch of stuff you bought last week. It might not hurt to fast, either. Remember how you hear Me better when you're fasting? Allow the Holy Spirit access to that anxiety building up inside you. Do it right now. Trust Me. I'll prompt you when it's a good time to shop. Now, let's go to the beach and talk."

I did, and peace returned. I tried coupling resets and fasting. Guess what? I did hear God's voice more clearly.

I'm sure you see the pattern here. My "gottas" were raising anxiety in my heart. They were crowding grief work out of my life. I found they were really "want-tos", not "gottas."

I learned to say, "I want to change the bed. It's overdue.

What do You say, Lord?" Usually, I'd be impressed to finish the grief work I was doing first. Then I could do the want-to task peacefully. Approaching to-dos this way lowered my anxiety level. It increased my peace quotient and prioritized my grief work. It also got the tasks done. Most importantly, it advanced my grief journey. It moved me through that "valley of the shadow of death" (Psalm 23:4, NASB). It was a true course correction. It was a bit painful at first as it took me time to settle into the new course.

§

A DIFFERENT KIND OF CORRECTION

I (Chris) identify with Job. I'm thankful I have wide margins in my Bible, as I have more personal notes in Job than any other book. I get his pain, emotions, and his cries to God. I get his cries *at* God. I really get Job's misunderstanding and his confusion. But what melts my heart is his own correction along the way.

That correction is beautifully expressed in Job 43:3–6 (NKJV).

Therefore, I have uttered what I did not understand. Things too wonderful for me, which I did not know. Listen please and let me speak. You said I will question You and You shall answer me. I have heard of You by the hearing of the ear. But now my eye sees You. Therefore, I abhor myself and repent in dust and ashes.

The word "repent" can be defined as "to turn around." It can mean "to change direction." It also can mean "to change the mind about or toward something." Sounds like some course correction was going on here with Job.

Early in the last couple of years of my wife Irene's life, the mental, emotional and physical toll was mounting. As her primary caregiver, so was my frustration. It had been a rough ten years. I had sought the Lord many times concerning her.

Irene would often cry out in pain, and ask me to pray "one more time please, to end this suffering." I had done so several times before.

God did answer, but not to my liking. His words to me were, "I know, I understand, and I am here." You would think they would be comforting words. But I wasn't connecting. I wasn't buying it, and I was getting angry. *It's nice You're here*, I thought, *but why don't You do something? I thought You were good. What happened to all this healing You're supposed to do? Why are You so silent? Why are You not telling me what's going on? Why can't we be free of this stuff? How come the more I pray, the worse things get? Hey, God, You gotta fix this.*

The course we were on continued for two more years. There was no change. Then . . . Irene died.

Then God really began to speak to me. It was like He suddenly appeared on the scene. I remembered He did that with Job. He said, "We need to talk." The first item on the list was about His goodness. "You are angry because you are thinking I'm not good. You base this upon your circumstances, expectations, and assumptions. You base it on your understanding of Me. It's about how and when I should do things."

I began to think about redemption. If any came, it would have to come from God. If any goodness at all came, He had to bring it. If I received any restoration, any healing, He would bring it. If there was any fixing of all this mess, God would fix it. In fact, He is the only one in the universe who can. He alone has the track record of doing just that. How could I be mad at Him? What I need from Him will not come from anyplace else. That makes Him really good.

"You, God, are ultimately good on my behalf," I confessed. "You will make even this stuff beautiful in Your time." My anger lifted. I was at peace. Correction number one.

Then, He began to deal with my beliefs about His sovereignty. I realized He does have a plan, and I have little choice but to surrender. When He is functioning from His sovereignty, I have the choice to take over. It's called rebellion. He reminded me that He was God, and I was not. Kind of like He did with Job, but with a lot more grace.

Then came this Scripture: "The secret things belong to the Lord our God, but those things which are revealed belong to us and to our children forever, that we may do all the words of this law" (Deuteronomy 29:29, NKJV). I learned a couple of lessons here.

First, there are things I will never know or understand. There are things I can't even begin to comprehend. They are secret to me, and they are known by God only.

Second, God is not under any obligation to tell me what these are. It's on a need-to-know basis. He simply said He was not going to tell me. "You don't need to know all the details of what Irene and you went through." His question to me was, "Are you going to be okay with it? Are you going to trust Me on this one?"

And this time, I responded, "Yes, Lord, I will." I settled into a restful place under His mighty hand. I was okay with it. Those things that have been revealed are sufficient for me. Correction number two.

Over the years I have asked the Lord about those details. I asked all the whys and what-fors. To this day, He has never told me one thing concerning the details of that season. I'm still okay with that. Oh, by the way, those three short sayings of His? They were the *perfect* answer for me. I just couldn't see it at the time. Now they make perfect sense. "I know, I understand, and I'm here."

My take-aways:

- I am at peace with a tremendously enlarged heart. I am rich and full—so full that I sometimes am unable to articulate it.
- God has brought order out of my chaos.
- I am greatly in love with Jesus as never before.
- I can walk through my grief journey with hope.

I have hope in a God who may not stop times of chaos in my life. He will always bring me through them, which is true even if the valley only ends at the gates of heaven. In the meantime, there really is a God. He, amid your brokenness or chaos, will also adjust, correct, or move upon you. It's all for your victory and His highest best for you. Jesus said, ". . . you may have peace. In this world you will have trouble. But take heart! I have overcome the world" (John 16:33).

DISCUSSION QUESTIONS

1. Times of suffering can also be times of new growth. In what ways do you feel the Lord is helping you grow?

_____

_____

_____

_____

_____

_____

_____

_____

_____

_____

2. Looking back on your life, what are some lessons you have learned from your loving heavenly Father? What are benefits you see in your life now that are results of painful past circumstances?

_____

_____

_____

_____

_____

_____

_____

_____

_____

3. Job had friends who gave him bad advice during a crisis. Have you ever had friends like that? Has someone falsely blamed you for the crisis? How did you respond?

_____

_____

_____

_____

_____

_____

_____

_____

_____

_____

_____

4. Grieving well takes time and energy. Often it takes a lot of time and energy. What are you doing to persevere in your grief journey? How do you respond when God prompts a course correction?

_____

_____

_____

_____

_____

_____

_____

_____

_____

_____

GROWING STRONGER GUIDELINE #8

Run Your Race

Remember, your victory is just around the corner.

CHAPTER EIGHT

Run Your Race

STRENGTHEN YOURSELF FOR THE RACE

*Let us run with endurance the race God has set
before us (Hebrews 12:1, NLT).*

*So take a new grip with your tired hands and
strengthen your weak knees. Mark out a straight path
for your feet so that those who are weak and lame
will not fall but become strong (Hebrews 12:12–13, NLT).*

TRAINING FOR THE RACE OF GRIEF

What is my race? How I (Bruce) run depends on the race I'm running. I've often heard, "Life is a marathon, not a sprint." That's true of the grief journey as well. So, our race is the one we're running together, guys. Marathons are brutal. How do the runners survive, let alone finish the race? How do they—wonder of wonders—win? They train hard, intensively, intentionally, and consistently. How do we men train to run the marathon of the widowed?

How am I to finish this marathon? How do I run it with endurance? To do it, I need those 12th and 13th verses above. I will have to take a new grip. That means change what I'm doing. I will have to strengthen my weak knees. There are places in me that are weak. They need some attention. That may require me to change as well. Finally, I'm to mark out a straight path for my feet. Here are some of the ways I can do all that.

GOOD SELF-CARE

Successful runners take good care of their bodies and souls. They care for their minds, their wills, and their emotions. So must I. And I need to pay attention to my spirit. It has been crushed (Psalm 34:18). I really need to:

- Get good nutrition—eat healthy food, drink plenty of clean water, and avoid unhealthy comfort or "junk" food.
- Get enough sleep—this facilitates taking a new grip. It strengthens weakened parts of the self. It aids in keeping a

clear mind to mark out a straight path.

- Get enough exercise—no problem for an athlete, as a rule. Often, it's a big problem for the widowed. Our want-to is gone and our schedule is chaotic. We may need another man to walk or workout with.
- Get enough quality time with God. How else will I know the straight path for me?
- Get enough quality time with my caring community. I've heard that "no man is an island." In grief, I've tried to be an island by isolating myself. When I've isolated, I've sunk into the sea of sorrow and had great difficulty getting to the surface again.
- Get enough recreation—I call it re-creation, because it recreates me from the inside out. It's just this simple. I like to hike the trails and mountains. I like to walk the beaches and sit there with Jesus. I like to sing praise and worship songs. I like to read good books. When I do these things enough, I move through that shadow valley of Psalm 23:4. If not, I don't.

All this is hard to do! At least, it was for me. My life was chaos— at least in the beginning it was. My want-to was gone. My to-do lists looked like books! Even so, I will tell you the truth, brothers in grief. It is doable. I'm doing it, and it works!

LET THE LORD SET THE PACE

In junior high and high school, I ran competitively on my school's cross-country teams. In our training and practice sessions, we attempted to find our race pace, the sustainable pace at which we finished best when racing, which really helped in competition. One strategy our opponents often employed was to designate one of their team as a "rabbit." This runner would leave the starting line in a sprint. He would keep up the pace until he was exhausted, unable to run. And so were any of our team who took the bait. If they tried to stay with him, they too became exhausted and were unable to finish. Knowing our own race pace kept us from taking that bait.

As a believer, I have another opponent. He's that one who comes only to rob, kill, and destroy me. He and his kingdom of darkness want to rob me. He would steal the blessings the Lord has for me. He wants to keep me from completing my grief journey. If possible, the kingdom of darkness would love to wear me out. It wants to discourage me and trap me in my grief. The solution for me is to stay close to the Lord. Then, I proceed in my grief work at the pace He sets. He keeps me from trying to sprint through the process.

RUN WITH COURAGE

I have tried to run this marathon at the Lord's pace. Still there were times when I have been tempted to give up. Grief ambushes me on tough days: Cheri's birthday, the anniversary of her passing, Valentine's Day, Christmastime, etc. Those days, I often feel like quitting.

On those days, it has helped me to remember what I once read in a greeting card: "Courage is not the absence of fear. It's going ahead anyway." That's what it means to run with endurance. That's how we do as the writer of Hebrews tells us.

In my cross-country career, I never won a single race. I never even placed second or third! I did finish every race. I believe that's what Jesus wants for us, guys. His interest is that we do finish our grief journey. It is not how fast we get through the process. To finish takes courage and endurance.

It is normal and natural for widowed believers to long for heaven. After all, we hope to see our wives again there. It is downright dangerous, however, if I begin to make plans—especially plans to get there sooner—especially if very soon. That is called suicide. That kind of thinking must be a red flag to all of us. This is especially true if it persists over time. That is the attempt of the kingdom of darkness to kill me. I love what Mary Beth says about this in *Don't Lose Heart!*

> This is a psychiatric emergency. Call 9-1-1. It's important for family and friends to stay connected with the widow so they can monitor changes in behavior. Suicide is *not* the way out! God promises hope! As 1 Corinthians 10:13 reassures us, "No temptation has overtaken you except what is common to mankind. And God is faithful; He will not let you be tempted beyond what you can bear. But when you are tempted, He will also provide a way out so that you can endure it." With the proper support of faith, family, friends, counseling, and medical care, widows can recover and return to the race.

Men, we can stay in the race too.

KNOW THE COURSE

At competitive cross-country races, no two courses are the same. Often, the visiting runners don't know the course at all. Prior to the start, race officials clearly mark the course. Then, they walk all the racers through the course. That way, the visitors know where the good places to pass are located. They'll know where the tight places are where they can lose ground if they're trying to pass. They also learn what the finish line looks like. They can mark in their mind a spot where they will start a sprint to the finish line.

Paul says in Romans 1:20 that the visible or created world helps us understand the invisible, spiritual world. So, here's how I unpack this section of the race metaphor. We learned early in my grief journey that no two grief journeys are alike. This is just like the cross-country courses.

We each grieve differently. As a visiting runner to this grief racecourse, I want to know where the official is who will lay out my course. When will he walk me through it? For me as a believer, that's easy. The race official is Jesus. He is right here in my heart. He will show me my course, step by step.

This is where my spiritual disciplines keep me tuned to the Lord. I stay sensitive to the twists and turns of the course. The Lord shows where those tight places are. He shows where potential grief ambush danger lurks. Knowing will help me prepare in advance for them. I'll not push myself too hard right then. Maybe I'll even fall back a little bit. I can regroup for a push later. Jesus and I can create a plan in advance. Following the plan will get me through that challenging place. Then, I'll be ready for the next phase of the race.

Isaiah 61:3 promises that God will give us the oil of joy instead of mourning and a garment of praise instead of a spirit of despair. Friends like Chris Taylor, years further into their race, reassure me. They tell me that the joy will come. I must just persevere and not give up.

FOLLOW GOD—STAY ON THE COURSE

If joy is our finish line, how do we get from here to there? In order to win this grief race, we must stay on course. Ephesians 5:1 tells us to "follow God's example, therefore, as dearly loved children." This is why I call the Bible, the "Life Owner's Manual." It is where I find the rules of the race and guidelines about the racecourse. And it's why the disciplines in Chapter 1 are so important for me. Many of these embed Scripture specific to the grief journey in my heart.

RUN *THROUGH* THE FINISH LINE!

When I was racing, there was a tape that marked the finish line. Our coach trained us to always lean—or leap—through that tape. That prevented us from easing up just before getting there. Easing up opens the door for an opponent who doesn't. That's what I'm doing when I focus on the joy God promises. He says He will convert my weeping into laughter, lavish comfort on me, and invade my grief with joy.

§

SEASON

I (Chris) like to use the term season to describe this thing we call grief. In the grief process, everything is so very individual. The journey is so very personal, so I don't want to project my personal experience into the general experience. What works for me may not fit another grieving person.

I was following God through trials, problems, commands, and conditions, as well as through blessings, mountaintop experiences and low-valley times. I was gaining a lot and learning a lot. The lessons were many and varied. God did not waste any of it. At the same time, His yoke was easy and His burden light. The purpose of it all was to be conformed to the image of Christ.

Then came the loss of Irene. It was like running smoothly in the 1500 then suddenly being hit with a hamstring pull. I'm not a runner, but I've seen the results of this type of injury. Roger is pastor of the Thorp Community Church. He was at youth camp playing Capture the Flag when he was hit with a hamstring pull. He showed me the black and purple bruises and damage to his leg the size of a dinner plate a couple days later. That was how grief affected me.

After Irene was gone, I was impressed with Jeremiah 29:11. It was as if God said to me, "I have plans for you. They will be specific to your season of grief. They will fit you perfectly. They will be easy to receive. You will have different disciplines and different results."

I found that grief needs to be embraced. That happens through the grace, love, and healing power of Jesus. It has a beginning and an end—mostly. The end is not sudden, as is finishing a race. Rather, it is fading from one season to another. It's so smooth I didn't even see it coming. In the grief season there is no one decisive moment when it's over. There is no tape at the end I can see or lean into. When can I say I have won?

One person said grief is like being in a major destructive earthquake. When it hits, it knocks you off your feet. At first you land really hard as your strong legs buckle and you fall to the ground. But then you draw close to Jesus because you know in that place He is close to you. Psalm 34:18 says it this way, "The Lord is close to the brokenhearted and saves those who are crushed in spirit."

Though your disciplines are available, at first you're not thinking of them. It's more like a tear-filled cry of "God help me!" than a discipline.

The next time the earthquake-like aftershock of grief hits is different. This time, the landing is just a little softer. The pressing into God still remains. When grief came again and again, over and over I cried, "Jesus, You're my only hope." It was Jesus and me; Jesus was carrying me when I couldn't stand.

I learned to be purposeful in my sorrow, looking for a way to let my pain and sadness come to the surface. I wanted to let it out as I longed for the comfort of Jesus, and He brought His comfort as only He can.

Watching the video of my wife's memorial service brought it all to the surface for me. As it touched me deeply, I ended up in a waterfall of tears. I did this again and again. I did it even when I didn't think I needed it. I really did, though. I poured out my grief and sadness to the Lord. He ministered His comfort every time. I didn't have to wait until the end of the season to collect. My reward in the season was immediately mine.

When I went to church, I would take a big wad of Kleenex in my pocket. As I opened my heart to the Holy Spirit, He met me every time. He touched my emotions with His comfort. He helped me take another step toward wholeness.

My season lasted close to four years, but the Lord Jesus brought me through. I learned plenty about Him, myself, and my growth. I land softly now. When the season was over, there was no big hurrah. There were no fireworks. There was no medal that said, "Well done, good and faithful servant." That will come later, by God's grace. What did come was contentment and peace. I had a sense that all was okay with me. I was with my Jesus who gave Himself for me. In that season, I fell deeply in love with Jesus. I was brought closer and deeper as I had never experienced before. This goes so deep it really is beyond human language to articulate it. I am eternally grateful to Him for my season.

Remember above where I said there is an end—mostly? Ten years later, it usually feels like all my mourning and sorrow have melted away. However, there can still be a remembrance that comes to the surface. This causes a small rumble. No big quakes here, but a feeling of "I just miss her." It's only momentary, and there is no real sadness. It may even evoke a little smile for the good times that were.

SUPPORT

I, like Bruce, put certain disciplines in my life that helped me stay in a good place in relationship with Jesus. Some started the day I received Christ as my Savior. Others were added later as I grew in the Lord. They were not difficult to keep and were, and still are, a joy in my life. I really like prayer, reading the Word, and worship. My disciplines include going to church, Bible study, being in a small group, and good self-care.

I never thought of these as disciplines, or rules to follow. I did hear from various pulpits that if I missed one, I was heading for disaster. Me? I was just loving Jesus. I was staying close to Him and doing His plan for me. I was following God. I was in the race for the crown that awaits me at my home-going to Jesus. This race never ends until then.

DISCUSSION QUESTIONS

1. Describe the habits that have helped you most along your grief journey.

   _____

   _____

   _____

   _____

   _____

   _____

   _____

   _____

   _____

   _____

   _____

   _____

2. What are you adding or eliminating from your lifestyle to make your journey better?

   _____

   _____

   _____

   _____

   _____

   _____

   _____

   _____

   _____

   _____

3. It can be very encouraging to train with other people. Who would you consider to be on your team in this race or season? In what ways do you support each other?

_____

_____

_____

_____

_____

_____

_____

_____

_____

_____

_____

4. If you could not answer the above question to your satisfaction, consider the importance of developing teammates. Bible studies, prayer groups, and support groups are a few ways to develop a support system. This is very crucial to a widowed person. What are some resources you could access to develop your support system?

_____

_____

_____

_____

_____

_____

_____

_____

_____

5. Chris' analogy of grief as a season for him, as opposed to a race, offers us a fresh perspective on the grief journey. What stood out as good ideas for you?

_____

_____

_____

_____

_____

_____

_____

_____

_____

_____

_____

6. How might that look as you adopt them into your own grief work?

_____

_____

_____

_____

_____

_____

_____

_____

_____

_____

_____

_____

Remember, God Is On Your Side

God's love is based on His love for you, not your performance.

CHAPTER NINE

God Is On Your Side

THE LORD IS FOR YOU!

Listen to me, you descendants of Jacob, all the remnant of the people of Israel, you whom I have upheld since your birth, and have carried since you were born. Even to your old age and gray hairs I am He, I am He who will sustain you. I have made you and I will carry you; I will sustain you and I will rescue you (Isaiah 46:3–4).

HOW MUCH DOES GOD LOVE ME?

I (Bruce) *love* personalizing Scripture! I have reworded Isaiah 46:3-4 this way: You have upheld me since my birth and have carried me since I was born. Even to my old age and gray hairs You are He, You are He who sustains me. You made me and You carry me. You sustain me and You rescue me.

It so convincingly answers the question, "How much does God love me?" My God has been with me since I was conceived! He made me who I am. He made me the way He wanted me to be. He has carried, sustained, and even rescued me. He has done it throughout my life, and He is always with me! Here's the really big deal: He won't do for me what He won't do for you. Do whatever you do to get close to Him, then ask, "How do You see me right now, Jesus?" And keep asking and listening. I know He loves to answer that question.

BUT I CAN'T FEEL HIM

In Chapter 9 of *Don't Lose Heart!*, Mary Beth Woll answers this objection well when she says, "Sometimes the effects of grief can keep you from 'feeling' the presence of God until you work through those memories. Often professional help is needed to do this."[13] This is tough for a lot of us guys. We don't easily ask for help.

I once received unsolicited professional help when I broke our car's windshield with my face in a head-on collision. It happened

---

13   Mary Beth Woll, MA, LMHC, Linda Smith, Paul Meier, MD, *Don't Lose Heart! A Widow's Guide To Growing Stronger* (The Widows Project, 2020), p. 69.

when I was a teen and before seatbelts, I must say. I was very grateful for the unsolicited professional help I received. It saved my life.

All of us have broken the windshields of our lives with our faces. The "windshields" I'm talking about are our *wives*. True or true? The difference here is that the damage isn't obvious. It's up to us— you and me—to admit, "Yes, I need help."

We must seek it when we get stuck in processing our loss. I did. It was hard to humble myself this way. I was raised, trained, and experienced in handling everything myself. I dealt with whatever came at me. I couldn't do it this time. When I got stuck and asked for help, it worked! God showed up and delivered. He used other members of Jesus' Body. I got unstuck and went off on my journey to joy. Please remember: God won't do for me what He won't do for you.

One of the main methods God used to help me is called Transformation Prayer Ministry (TPM). TPM is a tool for deep restoration. It is facilitated healing for wounds in the heart (see the Resources section at the back of the book for more on this).

In Chapter 4 I described the healing of a deep fear of death, a fear transmitted to me prior to birth. Healing of the fear preceded and led to my mind being renewed. It nearly always does. My mind gets stuck in a negative thinking pattern. It does this because my heart is wounded.

One of my negative thinking patterns went like this: "I'm a failure. I mess up everything I touch." The heart wound that caused it came from my angry dad. He said this to me: "You're never going to amount to anything. You're no son of mine. I disown you. Now get out, and don't come back!"

I believe God created every little boy to want his daddy's approval. I needed my dad's affirmation. The little boy in me died that day. Can you see it? My negative thinking pattern was linked to that heart wound. When Jesus healed the wound in my heart, my thinking could be transformed. Romans 12:2 describes this mind renewal process. The mind renewal followed in time, and wow!— the transformation in my life experience was profound. One of those life experiences was my relationship with my dad. It wasn't just restored. It was transformed, became stronger and more loving than ever!

Here's the point of this story: TPM is facilitated prayer. It requires me to ask for help. I've used many facilitated services in getting unstuck in my grief journey. Medical help, counseling, and grief recovery groups are facilitated services. I know it's hard, guys. It was for me. But it worked. Every time I asked for help, it came. Furthermore, I really believe what God did for me He will do for you.

IN THE GOOD TIMES/ IN THE BAD TIMES

Many times, pain causes folks to question God. It has caused many believers to ask, "If God is for me, loves me, and is all-powerful, why do bad things happen to me? Why do horrible things like being widowed happen to me?"

I have settled this for myself. John 10:10 tells me, "The thief [Satan] *comes only to steal and kill and destroy; I* [Jesus] have come that they may have life and have it to the full" (parentheses mine). That thief lost his authority on earth to Jesus. Jesus gave that authority to His followers. But that thief does still have power on earth—power to steal, kill and destroy. Jesus does not promise trouble-free living. He said, "In this world you will have trouble. But take heart! I have overcome the world" (John 16:33).

I love how the Classic Amplified Version describes the phrase "overcome the world": "I have deprived it of power to harm you and have conquered it for you." If you're struggling with asking for help, please pray into this. Persist. Ask, and keep on asking. Do it until you experience God's comfort, counsel, and peace.

As a matter of fact, that's my favorite tool to use whenever I'm struggling: ask and keep on asking. I ask God and my caring community and specialists in my struggle area. I ask until God's comfort, counsel, and peace come for me.

Here's some encouragement from one specialist: Author Barbara Johnson says, "Trial and triumph are what God uses to scribble all over the pages of our lives. They are signs that He is using us, loving us, shaping us to His image, enjoying our companionship, delivering us from evil, and writing eternity into our hearts."[14]

---

14 Worthy Inspired, *Overcoming Tough Times: God's Answer to Every Situation* (New York, Worthy Publishing, 2016), p. 25.

I've done my best to stay as close to Jesus as I can. In this grief journey, I have found the most profound and rapid growth of my life. I have grown personally, relationally, and spiritually. I call it an example of Jesus' conquering the world for me. And again, what God did for me, He can also do for you.

OVERCOMING OBSTACLES

I don't want it to sound like I have it all together. I have suffered as a result of my own poor choices. I have ignored offers for help. I have isolated myself from others. I have binged to numb the pain. I'm sure you see it. The bigger damage isn't usually in the initial failure. It comes when I stay there. Whenever I've gone to God and asked forgiveness, I have received it. It's also worked with anyone else I have hurt. They forgave me, and I also received strength to press on in the journey.

My reactions to the details of Cheri's illness and death included feelings of anger, resentment, fear, and guilt. TPM helped me resolve these distressing emotions. Removing these obstacles followed the same path that I've outlined in dealing with my fear of failure.

Another area that plagued me was feeling guilty about the relief I felt. I felt relieved when I was released from being Cheri's 24/7 caregiver. That work got very intense in the last three months of her life. I was very tired by the end. So much so that I didn't even realize how tired I was. My body did though—it kind of fell apart.

I also discovered that I resented Cheri. She quit doing some of the therapies I described in Chapter 1. These therapies had brought her cancer indicators into the "safe zone." She actually quit taking three important supplements. All three were known to minimize the risk of further attacks. She did this because "they cost too much." I felt guilty here too. I couldn't convince her to continue taking them. She just wouldn't do what her health care professionals prescribed and I resented her for that.

I've known of others who had painful marriages. They became resentful as a result. That resentment complicated their grieving process.

And I know of still others who have felt abandoned by a spouse who died by suicide.

All of these emotional responses in the grief journey can be handled similarly. I really like what Mary Beth Woll says to widowed women. I'll paraphrase it to apply to us men as well:

> In any of these cases of complicated grief, the widowed ones must first address the distressing emotions before they can move forward with the grief process. They may condemn themselves for having feelings that are different than other widowed folks, but when they realize that God is for them, not against them, they can count on Him to help them untangle their emotions. [15]

§

I (Chris) really like the above quote from Mary Beth. It assures me that God loves me and is for me. It assures me He will help untangle the emotions I feel in my grief. I needed to know He is for me.

When Irene passed away, my emotions were a mess. They, and my responses to them, were like a bowl of spaghetti—I couldn't separate them out for the life of me. I felt loneliness, anguish, anxiety, sorrow, guilt, apathy, abandonment, confusion, rejection, pain, anger, rage, and disappointment. I didn't know which were feelings, or assumptions, or beliefs. I didn't know which were true or just plain lies.

While taking a course in grief recovery, I described my grief as a hockey puck that was slammed around from one end to the other. Then I likened it to trying to swim upstream from the edge of Niagara Falls. I was over the edge and being sucked down again and again. There was no escape from the vortex. But I also knew God was loving me through the vortex. He was *for* me and I was not about to be destroyed. God had been faithful all my life. He had brought me through all sorts of experiences, and He would do the same now. I believed He would make this mess okay. The Lord dropped this little nugget into my heart: "He has made everything beautiful in its time" (Ecclessiastes 3:11).

Then there is Philippians 1:6 (NKJV): "Being confident of this very thing, that He who has begun a good work in you will complete it until the day of Jesus Christ." God is pro-Chris. He is pro-you, too, by the way. In fact, God was so *for* me that it was He who led me to

---

15   Mary Beth Woll, MA, LMHC, Linda Smith, Paul Meier, MD, *Don't Lose Heart! A Widow's Guide To Growing Stronger* (The Widows Project, 2020), p. 73.

grief recovery groups. Once there I reached out to God and people to help me. They got me through my season of grief. These three great truths became mine in that community:

- I was "normal" in the midst of my spaghetti tangles. That was a comfort.
- I was not alone. Twice the comfort there.
- This would eventually pass.

I jumped in all the way. Thank God that He cares enough to take leadership in my life. He has my best interests in mind. Thank God He will take this mess called grief and use every part of it. He will show me His love, care, presence, and how much He is *for* me.

In dealing with the pain of grief and sorrow, I have observed that our pain comes from three sources. All of them need the presence of the Holy Spirit to move through them. Please don't forget this. God is for you and will lead you through these things. Let's look at these three pain sources:

- **The loss and emotional responses of grief.**
  This is what I experienced in studying grief. God moved me through these by His love and care. He separated each from my spaghetti bowl as time went by. He and I figured out the bowl of spaghetti together. It eventually ended in freedom.
- **The residual pain that is expressed in those lingering issues that just won't go away.**
  These are like Bruce's issues with Cheri that limited his movement forward. My issues needed to be resolved, once and for all. In this place, professional help may be needed. Bruce's experience with Transformation Prayer Ministry (TPM) could also work well for you in this context.
- **Issues that were there all the time, but I didn't realize it.**
  The experience of grief brought them to the surface. I became *aware* of them. These issues were often quite deep. They had been around for a long time. They did not just show up in the grief process. These latent issues can have roots that are historic in nature. They may go back many years. A good TPM facilitator or other professional help could also be needed here. These latent issues definitely affected me even before I was totally aware of them.

It is the goodness and kindness of God to show us sources of our pain. Be vigilant here. The enemy of our soul would like to use pain to cripple us, but God will reveal our issues to heal us. God only works on the ones that He reveals at the time. It is good to work with someone experienced with ministering in these areas. Partnership with a well-prepared godly man is another expression of God's love for us. Often, we need a Jesus with skin on, and God provides what we need.

We (Bruce and Chris) remain confident in this: God, *our* God, *will* do for you what He has done for us.

DISCUSSION QUESTIONS

1. The passing of time can give us perspective on suffering. We don't have that perspective when we are in the middle of it. What do you see differently now that you didn't see previously?

_____

_____

_____

_____

_____

_____

_____

_____

_____

_____

_____

2. When we suffer unjustly, it can be tempting to retaliate. Jesus showed us a better way. He instructed us to turn the other cheek (Matthew 5:39). This is contrary to human nature. We fear if we do it, we will be injured further. In such cases, Jesus is our example. He said in John 10:18 regarding His own life, "No one takes it from me, but I lay it down of my own accord." This does

not mean that we subject ourselves to abuse. It is important to take steps that are necessary to be safe. What it *does* mean is that we do not return evil for evil. We are to return evil with blessing (1 Peter 3:9). How do these Scriptures apply to your grief journey?

_____

_____

_____

_____

_____

_____

_____

_____

_____

_____

3. One reason it can be so difficult to return good for evil is that we fear justice will not be done. In such cases, 1 Peter 4:19 urges us to commit ourselves to our faithful Creator. We are to continue to do good. We are to leave the injustice of the situation with God. We are to trust that He will heal our souls. He will do a much better job than we ever could! Are you struggling with an unjust situation? It might be an inheritance dispute, medical malpractice, or a family squabble. If so, pause now, note it here, and prayerfully commit the concern to the Lord. Do not hesitate to get professional help if needed.

_____

_____

_____

_____

_____

_____

4. What obstacles are you facing on your grief journey? What are the sources of these obstacles? Your most recent loss? Residual pain? Latent pain that came to the surface recently? List them here for future reference. The first step to removing a barrier is identifying what it is.

_____

_____

_____

_____

_____

_____

_____

_____

_____

5. Ask God to direct you as you work on your personal obstacles. Who else might you ask for help in dealing with them? List your impressions here for use later.

_____

_____

_____

_____

_____

_____

_____

_____

_____

_____

_____

Grieve with Company

Weep with those who weep until God wipes away all your tears.

CHAPTER TEN

Grieve with Company

TO COMFORT ALL WHO MOURN

*The Lord has sent Me to comfort those who mourn,
especially in Jerusalem. He sent Me to give them flowers in
place of their sorrow, olive oil in place of tears, and joyous
praise in place of broken hearts (Isaiah 61:2b-3, CEV).*

DOES GOD REALLY CARE?

When I (Bruce) was freshly widowed, I felt shattered. The question, "Why?" was continually swirling through my head and heart. I also asked, "Do You really care, God?" Now, four years later, I know by experience He *does* care. He not only cares, He also comforts and counsels.

As You said in Isaiah 61:2b-3, You really do comfort me when I mourn, Jesus. You give me flowers in place of my sorrow, olive oil in place of my tears, and joyous praise in place of my broken heart.

As I continued asking for it, He delivered that comfort and counsel faithfully. Psalm 56:8 (MSG) reads, "You've kept track of my every toss and turn through the sleepless nights, each tear entered in Your ledger, each ache written in Your book."

There it is. He not only *cares* about my pain, He keeps a record of it!

JESUS CARES!

Jesus said, "Blessed are those who mourn—they will be comforted" (Matthew 5:4, TPT). Not, "should," "might," or "could"; they *will* be comforted. Jesus promises we will. I love this next version because it helps me understand that first word in the passage. It reads, "Blessed and enviably happy [with a happiness produced by the experience of God's favor and especially conditioned by the revelation of His matchless grace]" (Matthew 5:4, AMPC). Now, let's stop here and consider that. Mourners are to be considered *"enviably* happy" and have *"experience* of God's favor?" Whoa! Now *that* challenges some of what I thought I knew about mourning.

Here's how the Lord fulfilled that particular promise to me: I described my morning walkie-talkies and afternoon resets in Chapter 1. During those times, there have been frequent tears. They came amidst verbal outpourings of my heart to God. Without fail, when I remember to ask, He has brought me comfort. Sometimes He does it even if I forget to ask! Sometimes the comfort is wildflowers along the trail. Other times, I feel a very present kind of presence. That presence holds me while I weep. And sometimes joyous praise does indeed pour out of my mouth. It comes in spite of my still-broken heart. The Holy Spirit has been my number one Comforter when the grief waves come. He knew I would need one. So, He gave me a second comforter also.

DUNCAN

He was supposed to be Cheri's dog. Duncan came home to us on Labor Day weekend in 2017 when he was two months old. You could have lit up a small city with Cheri's smile that day. She only got to enjoy him for a couple of months before she began requiring hospitalizations. Duncan went to live with Cheri's sister Vicky and her two adult daughters. I treasure the memory of those nieces smuggling Duncan into the hospital. They brought him to say goodbye to Cheri some six weeks later.

Once Cheri was gone, Duncan came home with me. For months, I suffered frequent bouts of weeping. The grief waves were huge and came often. At those times, Duncan could be playing in another part of the house or asleep in his den. Somehow, he would sense my weeping and come to where I was. He'd get up in my lap and stay until I was done weeping. When I stopped, off he went about his business. Very often, he would try to lick the tears from my face. Then, he settled in to calmly keep me company. Now full grown, he weighs nearly thirty pounds and is a solid lapful. Then he was only fifteen to twenty pounds and still had his incredibly soft puppy hair. To say he comforted me is a serious understatement! Duncan's puppy kisses were surely "olive oil" for my tears. Here's my point: Jesus, who created Duncan, built that into him. He did it for me! He saw me in my grief swirl before it happened. He knew what I would need and delivered!

How about the "joyous praise" part of that key verse? Usually,

Duncan and I play ball at some time every day. He has developed amazing ball-catching skills. Over the shoulder on a dead run fifteen yards out? Snatch! Easy. Four legs off the ground lunging for a high one? Speared! Doing a 180⁰ turn in the air in order to grab a tricky hop? You'd better believe it! At least once a day Duncan makes a spectacular catch, and I just have to jump up and shout with pleasure.

Duncan is an incredible locator as well. Here's another one of our games: while we are walking in the forest, I throw a ball or a stick as hard as I can off-trail into the brush. Invariably, Duncan finds it and brings it back to me. Sometimes he misses the direction of the throw. We've developed a set of hand signals I use to help him. He follows my signals to find the right general area to search. He swims through thorny thickets, and yes, in the lake, or salt water too. He almost always brings it back to me. Often, he earns my amazement and laughter. Sometimes the laughter comes right after tears. And, oh! How that joyous praise heals my broken heart! Jesus built those abilities into Duncan. He could see I'd need them. As Hagar said in Genesis 16:13, He is indeed "the God who *sees* me"!

The big deal here is not necessarily that you get a dog. I do recommend it, though. I would happily introduce you to Duncan if you'd like to explore the idea. Actually, the big deal here is to brag about Jesus. I want you to see how personal and intimate Jesus is. This is what He did in fulfilling His promise to comfort me. He was personal and intimate for me. He'll be that for you too. You must stay alert. His comfort wasn't always what I thought I needed. I actually resisted getting a dog. Jesus' comfort was always "more than I asked for or imagined" (Ephesians 3:20).

§

CUSTOM-MADE COMFORT

This is a fantastic thought. I (Chris) like the emphasis on the word *will* be comforted in Matthew 5:4. Apparently, there is no other option for our Lord to entertain. It's part of His business to do just that. It's a promise and also part of who Christ is.

The example of Duncan is amazing. As I meditated on it, another Scripture came to mind. 2 Corinthians 1:3 (NKJV) says, "Blessed be the God and Father of our Lord Jesus Christ, the Father of mercies, and God of all comfort." Did you catch that little word "all"? It prompts a question. Just how far will our heavenly Father go to bring me His promised comfort?

Irene, my wife of thirty-eight years, had been in failing health for years. She wanted to go home to heaven. So, in the middle of the night, she did. One of the deeply felt questions I had was, "Is she okay?"

A few days later the Lord gave me His answer. It was a picture, vision, or a vivid thought, I'm not sure which. In this impression, I saw a young and healthy Irene running up a grassy hill. I couldn't see over there, but I just knew that's where Jesus was. As she turned toward me, she wore one of the most joy-filled expressions I can remember. I had never seen *that* smile on her face before. Irene looked ecstatically happy.

She said to me, "I'm okay, don't worry about me. I want you to go and live life to the fullest. I don't need you anymore." She then continued up the hill out of my sight.

I'm not one who gets pictures or visions like that often. That scene brought peace, release and joy beyond my comprehension. It is so imprinted on my mind I shall never forget it. Neither will I forget the wonderful feeling of comfort around it. There would be more times of mourning on my grief journey. But right then, that moment was just what I needed. It was truly more than I thought, truly beyond my imagination. God really is the God of *all* comfort.

I'm not saying to search for some kind of vision or picture. I'm not saying to get a puppy, either. I will say, after experiencing Duncan, I'll agree with Bruce, a dog is not a bad idea. Here's the main point: Jesus walks closely with us in our grief. He cares deeply for each of us. He knows us. He will do whatever it takes. We will be comforted according to His promise. When He does, it will be just what we need. It will fit perfectly in our hearts and minds. This comfort is custom-made, and it just doesn't get any better. After facilitating grief groups several times, I learned something. This sort of custom comfort is not at all uncommon. Just be open to share your heart with Jesus. Allow Him to do what only He can do to comfort you.

GRIEVE IN COMMUNITY

We've said it before, and we'll say it again. It's *that* important. Yes, there really is a kingdom of darkness that would like to steal the healing power of grieving in community. That is especially true of us believers. It hates us, it hurts us, and it will kill us. It will do it any way it can. Killing the hope we find in a caring community by keeping us out of it? That is just too simple for our enemy not to try.

Be especially aware of your self-talk. Look for thoughts that disagree with who God made you to be. He made us to live best as part of a community. If you have thoughts such as, "I don't feel like going tonight, I don't think they really like me anyway," or "I'm not getting that much out of it," please, get ready and go to your small group, your online fellowship, or your Bible study. Attend your grief group, walking, biking, or biker group. Attend wherever you find your caring community. All the grief experts agree that isolation hurts us; community heals us.

I (Chris) would like to share a focus on what Bruce has called caring groups or communities. Sometimes group members may not have experienced grief themselves. The good thing is that they *have* experienced *you*. Depending on the group, some amount of transparency may be in order. You will find groups that will offer growth in Jesus for all. They will understand that grieving is not the whole of your life. They will see it *is* definitely a part of it right now. They will learn to respond accordingly. In Galatians 6:2 (KJV) it's called "bearing one another's burdens."

I remember a time when I was overcome by emotion in the middle of a men's Bible study. I was co-leading the group and suddenly I was ambushed. It wasn't a big one, but it was enough to stop me immediately. I even shed a tear or two. I had not been open with a lot that was going on, but some of the men did know. My co-leader took over the meeting and offered a bit of background that explained this emotion. Although some didn't understand, some did, and all were supportive. Then we went on with the Bible study.

Transparency like this builds greater community and openness with others and can be a powerful part of your healing process. If not connected, get connected if at all possible. If you are connected, stay connected.

§

Pass it On!

In 2 Corinthians 1:4–5 (TPT), we find one of God's "whys" for comforting us: "He always comes alongside us to comfort us in every suffering so that we can come alongside those who are in any painful trial. We can bring them this same comfort that God has poured out upon us."

We are comforted so that we can do likewise. When we do this, both giver and receiver get the comfort! That's God's economy, after all. The way to get more of something is to sow it as seed. A change happens for the mature believer. As I (Bruce) was growing in faith, my job was to receive nourishment. When I mature, if I continue to take without giving, it produces spiritual stagnation and toxicity in me, which I can then pass on to others. To grow, I must give from my heart.

The same is true of the grief journey. It is said that to heal fully, I must help someone else. Here are a few practical suggestions for how to give from your heart to others who are grieving:

1. Respond to a loss with a visit, a phone call, a card or a letter. The mourner may especially treasure written notes for a long time.
2. Offer to attend a *Take Courage!* or *Take Heart!* study group with him.
3. Lead a *Take Courage!* or *Take Heart!* study group yourself.
4. Stephen Ministries has an excellent series of four devotionals entitled *Journeying Through Grief.* These little books are designed to be given as gifts quarterly during the first year of loss. You can order the books or learn more about them at *https://www.stephenministries.org/*.

Don't worry if you don't know what to say to a grieving person. Many times, your very presence, a hug, or a shared tear is enough. It's enough to express that you care. "Weep with those who weep" (Romans 12:15, NKJV).

1. Reassure the mourner that grieving is a necessary part of his recovery.
2. Listen compassionately to the grieving man. Invite him to express his thoughts and feelings. He may especially want

to talk about his wife.

3. Don't be afraid to talk about the deceased loved one. Share encouraging memories.

4. Don't say, "Let me know if there's anything I can do to help." Instead, offer specific, practical assistance. Perhaps offer to help make a list of help he needs.

5. Remember that he will need support for months to come. Grieving takes time.

6. Assure him of your prayer support during his grief.

Giving comfort to other widowed guys is another way we can *grieve with company.* We hope you have found some new ideas for your own journey through grief here.

Discussion Questions

1. A Honduran proverb says, "Grief shared is half grief; joy shared is double joy." God knows we need others when we are grieving, which is why Romans 12:15 says, "Rejoice with those who rejoice; mourn with those who mourn." Which family, friends, ministers, or helpers are part of your grief support system? Who are the people who offered to help?

_____

_____

_____

_____

_____

_____

_____

_____

_____

_____

_____

_____

2. Consider joining a support group to process your grief. Christian support groups, such as The Widows Project, meet in churches or Zoom groups. Secular grief groups can be helpful, but they do not offer hope in Jesus. Don't isolate. Be proactive. You could check the internet for grief groups that meet near you. Write your next step here.

_____

_____

_____

_____

_____

_____

_____

_____

_____

_____

_____

3. Describe your pain and share it honestly with God. When possible, share it with trusted friends. Remember, "Blessed are those who mourn, for they will be comforted" (Matt. 5:4). List those friends here.

_____

_____

_____

_____

_____

_____

_____

_____

GROWING STRONGER GUIDELINE #11

Let Your Light Shine

Grow stronger through your loss
and become a blessing to others.

CHAPTER ELEVEN

Let Your Light Shine

YOUR TRANSFORMATION BRINGS GOD GLORY

*They will be called "Trees of Justice," planted by the Lord to
honor His name. Then they will rebuild cities that have
been in ruins for many generations (Isaiah 61:3b–4, CEV).*

A CONTINUATION

Journeys proceed along a path step by step. Scripture often shows me (Bruce) a path to follow in my grief journey. At the end of Chapter 10, we were looking at moving forward, and discussed moving from receiving comfort from others to giving comfort to others.

Now we begin to look at entering a larger sphere of influence. We'll discuss moving beyond being comforters of the widowed. Let's look at becoming champions of the widowed.

GOD IS THE GARDENER

The verses above make it clear that God has planted us. He did it to honor His name. I think of a tree as something very solid. Trees are often deeply rooted. If they are, they can withstand whatever comes at them—often for centuries. The only way I can imagine myself doing that is to sink my roots deep into the soil where the Gardener planted me.

We are trees of justice, so what is God's justice? Isaiah 1:17 (CEV) has it this way: "Learn to live right. See that justice is done. Defend widows and orphans and help those in need."

WE ARE THE REBUILDERS

Widows and orphans are "cities that have lain in ruins for many generations" (Isaiah 61:4, CEV). They need a champion to spearhead their rebuilding. They need a Nehemiah, a Joshua, perhaps even a David. I am drawn to that ruined city inhabited by other widowed men like me. I have given myself to rebuilding that city. I believe it's God's intention for me to do that. I'm committed because I received comfort from the Lord

(2 Corinthians 1:3), and I'm committed in order to honor His name (Isaiah 61:4). Please ask God if He would have you join me.

BEAUTY FOR ASHES

In Isaiah 61:3, the Lord has promised to give grievers beauty for ashes. That's a miracle. In all the miracles I recall, the Lord played the biggest part. But the miracle recipient referred to in Isaiah 61 always has a little something to do. So how do I participate in this particular miraculous exchange? Pastor Rick Warren offers a clue when he says, "Your greatest ministry will likely come out of your greatest hurt."[16]

I best understand my ministry as the work I do to express God's purpose for my life. My greatest hurt was losing Cheri. I regard my contribution to this book, as well as my other work with The Widows Project, to be my attempt at producing my greatest purposeful life work. This beauty for ashes exchange came out of my greatest hurt.

AMBUSHED!

It can happen at any time, and often comes as a surprise. I guess that's what makes it an ambush—the surprise of it. Here's how it happened to me today:

It was to be a big workday for me. I was to meet, via Zoom, with other widowed men in Latin America, to study *Don't Lose Heart!*. The meetings are largely in Spanish, which taxes me mentally because I am very out of practice speaking and thinking in Spanish. In addition, there's the emotional part. Sharing with twenty other widowed guys for a few hours takes a lot of energy! We share our stories and encouragements. That amplifies the emotional part for me. So many of the men are like me in so many ways! I am truly learning to "weep with those who weep" (Romans 12:15, NASB).

When I got up this morning, it was snowing heavily. I had expected it as snow was in the weather forecast. I had prepared for it by buying a new snow shovel and some ice melting crystals. However, I was unprepared for what it triggered in my heart. It doesn't snow much where I live.

When Cheri was alive, snow was an excuse for extra time together. We might snuggle some or read to each other by the fire.

---

16   Rick Warren in *Overcoming Tough Times: God's Answer to Every Situation* (New York, Worthy Publishing, 2016), p. 95.

Often, we'd go out to play in the snow for a bit. We *always* did if we were hosting grandchildren! In so many of our snow-day photos, we look very happy. Those images began to parade through my mind.

Then, too, there's this thing called "cellular memory." It works like this: my very cells "remember" Cheri. They remember the handholding, the snuggling and such. And they grieve the loss of all of that in their own way. Often when this happens, my tears flow freely. However, I have no words to describe the pain.

In the midst of my preparations for today's group, I was ambushed when all of these memories jumped on me. It's counter-productive to attempt to ignore or fight the waves of grief. This time I chose to interrupt my meeting prep. I spent some time with old photos and handkerchiefs. When the grief wave passed, I went back to preparing for my meeting.

The point is, we don't need to wait until we have it all together. We can start giving to others while we process our grief. Giving is not only part of the maturation process. It's also part of the healing process.

§

So, Let It Shine!

I (Chris) like the way Jesus clarifies things about light. First, He says, "I am the light of the world" (John 8:12). Then He flips it over and says, "You are the light of the world" (Matthew 5:14). Then there is the act of letting that light shine. I still remember teaching our children that little chorus, "This Little Light of Mine." The truth is that it just wasn't their little light that was shining. Mine was shining too.

Over the years, I found that my little light changed quite a bit. Most often it changed and increased. Amidst my ups and downs, trials and tests, grief and sorrow invaded my life. I had to learn to process these invasions. Part of the processing was progressing through them. That required the grace of almighty God. I kept asking Him, "How do I function with 'this little light' in the middle of all this stuff?"

"Let it shine!" Jesus says.

There are three things that could make all our lights shine brighter during our season of grief and mourning. The first is *authenticity.* A certain amount of transparency needs to surface and be demonstrated. Some may call it "just being honest." I'm honest about where I am in the process. I'm also fearless to let it show. If we aren't real with each other, it will be evident quickly. Then the effectiveness of the interaction vanishes. Authenticity is an essential when letting your light shine. I like what Bruce said earlier: "It's unnecessary to wait until we have it all together to start giving." If I share with authenticity, even my little light will be an encouragement to others. Though not fully developed, my light can minister to widowed people individually and in community.

Second, as I mature, my light will shine brighter. James 1:4 (NKJV) says, "But let patience have its perfect work that you may be perfect and complete, lacking nothing."

When I was a young preacher in my first church, I was asked to facilitate a funeral and a graveside ceremony. I knew all about how to do it. I even knew the steps involved in grieving. Afterward, I saw the widow standing in the middle of a supermarket weeping and wearing a lost, blank stare. I had no idea how to minister to her. I tried but I was not very successful. Kindly, she said, "It's okay; you just don't understand." She was right. I didn't. Later, I grew in empathy, understanding, and expertise in ministering to grievers. But even then, I was often ineffective because I hadn't experienced grief myself. I needed real-life experience to mature me.

J. Vernon McGee, a well-known radio Bible teacher, told of an older preacher and a younger man who were sitting side by side listening to an even younger preacher. He preached well. The younger man said, "Isn't this guy great?"

The older preacher replied, "Yes, he is good, but he is not *great.*"

"What makes you say that?" the young man asked.

"Because" said the older preacher, "he hasn't suffered yet."

After graduating, I told the dean of our Bible school that I would like to teach. He said something that has stayed with me through the years. "No, that would not be right. What you have now is mostly theory. You need some years of application and experience first. Then come and teach."

Don't underestimate the quality of ministry that comes with experience. Your light will shine brighter and brighter as you practice. Let this maturing do its perfect work in you.

My third point is found in what Jesus said in Matthew 5:14 (NKJV): "A city that is set on a hill cannot be hidden." Notice the word "cannot." That's right, you are already a light on a hill to be seen by others. Jesus put you there. The grief, sorrow, trial, or test that you experience makes all the difference. I have heard it said this way: "There is no real-life testimony without the test, which most do not particularly enjoy."

Just rest in being the city which cannot be hidden. Jesus will often orchestrate how you will be seen. You may minister in The Widows Project or another grief recovery group. This will develop maturity, expertise, and clarify your calling. Or maybe you'll just be someone who has been through it before and are ready to simply let your light shine. If the day comes when you see an older woman standing in the middle of the supermarket silently weeping with a blank stare, you'll know what to do.

Jesus told us, "You are the light of the world . . . let your light shine before others, that they may see your good deeds and glorify your Father in heaven" (Matthew 5:14,16). God has a purpose for each one of us—good deeds for us to do (Ephesians 2:10).

§

I (Bruce) asked Him, "What's my purpose right now, God?" I asked repeatedly throughout my grief journey. For over two and a half years, the impression I had was, "Stay close to me, process your grief, cry your tears. That's your job right now." Then one day the impression changed; "Comfort others with the comfort you yourself received" (2 Corinthians 1:3). It is because of the comfort I have received that I am sharing these thoughts right now.

I invite you to do that yourself. Ask, "What's my purpose right now, God?" Ask and keep on asking. His purpose for you may also change over time. I am convinced He will answer as only He can. Then the rest is up to you. Please let your light shine. The world needs you and your unique light.

DISCUSSION QUESTIONS

1. Describe people from the Bible who were transformed after being broken and became displays of God's splendor. What were they like before and after?

_____

_____

_____

_____

_____

_____

_____

_____

_____

_____

_____

_____

2. Have you, or anyone you know, gone through this transformation process? If so, please share the before and after story.

_____

_____

_____

_____

_____

_____

_____

_____

_____

_____

3. In the middle of your grief, remember that God has invested the very life of His Son on your behalf to bring you through to the other side. This is not only for your encouragement, but also for His glory! Reconsider Romans 8:32: "He who did not spare His own Son, but gave Him up for us all—how will He not also, along with Him, graciously give us all things?" Take a moment to thank God for His sacrifice of Jesus Christ. Then ask Him specifically for the help you need.

    _____

    _____

    _____

    _____

    _____

    _____

    _____

    _____

    _____

    _____

    _____

    _____

Leave A Legacy

When you glorify God through your grief, you become an example that will encourage generations to come.

CHAPTER TWELVE

Leave A Legacy
REBUILDING THE GENERATIONS

*They will rebuild the ancient ruins and restore the places
long devastated; they will renew the ruined cities that have
been devastated for generations (Isaiah 61:4).*

REBUILD THE RUINS

One of the places long devastated, is the tradition of a father's blessing. I (Bruce) translate blessing as "power to prosper," in every sense of the word. In ancient Israel, a father's blessing was part of the culture. This blessing was prized and sought after. At every Shabbat meal, the patriarch of the family would empower each member of the family with spoken words.

He would say things like, "My sweetheart Cheri, you have empowered me to prosper this week. You are my Proverbs 31 girl. You have engineered peace, health, and growth in our family in these ways . . ."

And, "Michael, my beloved son, you are named for an archangel. Like him, you are powerful in the ways of the kingdom of light. You bring love, inspiration, provision, and joy to my heart and to the rest of our family."

There were also ceremonies, like the Bar Mitzvah, designed to bring directional messages of encouragement to children at key times in their lives. All of our family members today would also benefit from such messages.

THEY'RE WATCHING YOU

Your families are grieving too—each of the members in their own way. They are watching how you handle your loss. You can show them how you run to God for comfort, counsel, and direction. Living honestly and openly before them will teach your kids more than anything you say to them. When our kids were grown, we realized that they had learned more by watching us than they did by what we told them. Our examples will live on after us.

LEAVE A REMEMBRANCE

Author Barbara Johnson says, "The difference between winning and losing is how we choose to react to disappointments."[17] In this spirit, I'd like to share a couple of things our family did. We wanted to leave a meaningful remembrance of Cheri.

Cheri asked that her cremains be scattered on a particular beach in one of our local parks. She called it "my peaceful place." From the time they were small, she brought the kids there. Now they bring their kids there. Cheri loved her family, and we loved her. She asked that we gather on her next birthday after her passing. We did the scattering, shared memories of her, and had a meal together. The park allowed us to install a memorial, a beautiful picnic table with a bronze plaque commemorating her life in a forest glade just above the beach. That's where we had our meal and time of remembrance. Now this beach has also become *my* peaceful place. I do many of my afternoon resets there, and I've done a lot of grief processing there. I have seen many families enjoying a meal together at the table. Cheri would have absolutely loved it.

LEAVE A LEGACY

How do you want to be remembered? Please consider this question prayerfully. In Chapter 11, we challenged you to ask, "What is my purpose right now, God?" The answer you received could reveal some of *His* perspective concerning your legacy.

Around 2000, Cheri and I began over fifteen years of work with Family Foundations International. This organization offers a variety of resources ranging from seminars and small group studies to books and recordings. All are designed to enable us to do family better. We began as participants in the seminars. Then, we trained as small group facilitators. Then we became presenters of seminars. We finally became trainers of other presenters. That work transformed our lives. Through this transforming work that was only interrupted by Cheri's passing in 2017, I recognized I had not been the kind of husband or dad I wanted to be.

One of the things we learned to do was a paternal blessing ceremony. We did one of these for each of our four adult sons. For their day, each son got to write the guest list. He chose the menu

17   Barbara Johnson in *Overcoming Tough Times: God's Answer to Every Situation* (Worthy Publishing, 2016), p. 58.

for the meal we cooked for the gathering. We sent out personalized invitations to each on the list. Each invitation included a note letting the invitee know that they would be given time to mention what they admired about our son.

Each of my blessing presentations was highly individualized for each son. Here are some of the common elements:

- I researched and read the meaning of their names and explained how I saw that son living out both the literal and motivational aspects of their names.
- Each received a custom-printed and framed document detailing this.
- I publicly owned, apologized for, and asked their forgiveness for the ways I had failed them as their dad.
- I told each one what uniquely made me proud to be their dad. I detailed the strengths I saw operating in their lives.
- Each received a gift from Cheri and me. It was something we felt best represented who they are to us. I explained the "why this gift" to the assembled family and friends.
- For those receptive to prayer, I prayed a father's blessing over them. For the others, I simply spoke it aloud without addressing it to God.
- Over the meal, we steered the conversation to include more what-I-like-about-this-guy stuff. We involved as many of the guests as were willing to share.

In the months and years following these events, our relationship with each of these sons deepened and intensified. Old rifts in relationships were mended. We were included more and more in the lives of their separate families. They also began including each other in more of their own family's activities. For example, we began annual family camping trips. The grandchildren began having sleepovers at each other's homes. In short, our family's life was transformed. We sowed some legacy into each of their hearts.

Celebrating a paternal blessing ceremony is just one of the ways Cheri and I learned to leave a legacy for our family. You can learn more if you'd like at *www.familyfoundations.com*.

§

MY JOURNEY: A PERSONAL NOTE

I (Chris) am ten years past the loss of my wife. I have *passed through* the journey of this loss. Accordingly, my perspective is vastly different from one who is in the middle of his journey. My journey consumed a large amount of my time, energy, emotions, and thoughts, but it has now faded into the background. I give it only an occasional, thoughtful remembrance.

I once heard a preacher say the grief and sorrow that we feel today will not be the capstone of our walk with Jesus. Easy for him to say! We might tell ourselves, "This is the worst ever of things I have had to go through." However, I have found that my life has been a series of worst things ever. There may even be a few more to experience.

The real questions are, "What is the legacy I leave after my grief season? What of substance is deposited in my heart and life? What could I use to leave a legacy of blessing for others?"

We will leave a legacy that will be there for all to see, but we can choose what it will look like. Maybe we need to take some time to consider just what was left behind in us when our grief journey was over.

I don't think it will be how well I did in my journey. I did well on some of it, but not so well on other parts. Quite frankly, I'd give myself a C-minus on a portion of it. Thank God I don't get to write my own report card. There is only One who can. I don't think I deserve to be remembered for how bravely or stoically I embraced my loss. I did not. And probably not even for how hard I worked and pressed into it, though I did.

Knowing about another's journey may encourage others to face their own losses. I sincerely hope so. It's a good legacy to pass on to others. My heart is clear here. I gave it my best shot to walk closely with my Jesus through it all. Then, again, I've always done that since I came to know Him.

The ones to evaluate this portion of my legacy more accurately are those who watched me, who have been closest to me in the journey, and who know the real me. They see past the thin veneer that we all present. I am grateful for the co-authoring privilege I share. I'm thankful to pass on some of my experience. I have done it multiple times. *That* is leaving a legacy, I think. I hope that those closest to me (family, friends, Christian brothers and sisters) see something more—much more. Building our legacy is ongoing until Christ returns, or we go home to be with him.

My wife Carmen and I think of legacy more often these days. Our maturing age may have something to do with it. The Holy Spirit gave her this inspiration after a Bible study:

Legacy

We all leave a legacy. None will be greater than the legacy of Jesus Christ . . . for His legacy is still being lived through His Holy Spirit in and through you and me. Travelers through that legacy journey may be well known or not, but we travel together if we travel with our Lord Jesus Christ.[18]

It is humbling to remember the nuggets of wisdom received during my grief journey. The true legacy placed in me is the legacy of Christ Himself. We magnify what we focus on. I now focus not just on getting through the grief. I include focus on the continuing mercy and grace of God throughout my life. What do you believe is your portion of God's mercy and grace?

Scripture says in Psalm 23:6 (NKJV): "Surely goodness and mercy shall follow me all the days of my life." In 2 Corinthians 12:9 (NKJV) we read, "My grace is sufficient for you." The apostle Paul also said it this way in 1 Corinthians 15:10 (NKJV): "By the grace of God I am what I am and His grace toward me was not in vain, but I labored more abundantly than they all, yet not I but the grace of God which was with me."

God increased my understanding of grief. He increased my ability to press into Him. He broadened the revelation of who He is. He expanded my understanding of who I am now after my loss. I am indeed greatly humbled. Much of what I gained has become part of my legacy. That legacy is bigger now after my journey from mourning to joy. Some was added during the journey, but most was added after I came out on the other side.

Some of the things are beyond my mind to grasp. Yet they are real, heart-expanding and full of love. I didn't have them in me before, so I must have received them somewhere along the journey.

---

18   Carmen Taylor.

The Author is Jesus, and He wrote into me all of who I am. He wrote into me what I have become. He gave the insights that I share. He gave me the counsel that others embrace when I share it. The more like Jesus I become is all from Christ Jesus. I am *His* legacy. I hope to pass it on in all I do.

How do you want to be remembered? I suppose we all could generate quite a list. But seriously, if you had to reduce the list to one saying, what could it possibly be? I would like to quote two godly men whom I highly respect.

The first is Pastor Whitman who led the Methodist church in Astoria, Oregon for many years. He was retiring and was asked, "How do you want to be remembered?" His response was not about his accomplishments—which were numerous—nor was it about how well he did with the congregation. His response was, "I would like it to be remembered that I was a Christian." At that time, around 1960, *Christian* meant something richer and deeper than it does these days. I believe that would be a great legacy.

The other quote is from Pastor Paul Zettersten who was a well-known pastor, preacher, and teacher here in the northwestern United States. He passed away at age 99 in December of 2021 after seventy-seven years of ministry. I heard him say this in the late 70s when I was attending Bible college. When facing a serious medical issue, he was asked about his legacy. His response, as I remember it, was, "Did I do my best for Jesus?" That was the bottom line of his legacy.

I was invited into building a legacy of life's journey with Jesus Christ many years ago when I accepted Him as Lord and Savior. Through the grace and mercy of almighty God, Jesus continues to build my legacy. Since then, God's goodness and mercy have followed me, and His grace has been sufficient.

You are invited to build that same legacy—the legacy of your journey with Jesus Christ through grief and sorrow and all of life's experiences. Sometimes life is a battle, also called tough work, but through it all we can remember He will never leave us nor forsake us (Deuteronomy 31:6).

Some of you may have meditations, inspirations, and songs given you throughout your legacy-building journey. Here is one of mine, a song:

In Your Presence, Oh, My King

When I think it's hard to feel Your presence, oh, my King,
and I falter at the hope of reaching You,
Then I choose by faith to come to You,
and I know I'll be touched when I press through.
Now I stand in Your presence, oh, my God and King
to worship You in humble adoration.
Now I know that I'm healed in all my heart and soul,
by the power of Your Spirit moving through me.
Now I bow with lifted hands to give You praise,
for I'm made whole in Your presence, oh, my King.[19]

When I think about what matters in life, and the legacy I want to leave, at the end of my life I want to answer a wholehearted yes to the question, "Did I live my life for Him?" Living for Him is a joyful adventure when I think about how good He is, and how faithful He has been to me all my life.

CHILDREN ARE OUR ARROWS!

We'd like to end *Take Heart!* with a quotation from *Don't Lose Heart!*

When I (Mary Beth) was nineteen years old and feeling sad from a major disappointment, my very wise father comforted me with this thought: "When an archer shoots an arrow, the farther back he pulls the bow, the farther the arrow will travel." Although I didn't really understand it at the time, I now see that as Christians we can yield to the Archer who will take what seems to be a setback and use it to "shoot us" farther than we ever would have gone had that setback not occurred.

Psalm 127:4–5 says that children are a reward and a heritage from the Lord. It goes on to say that they are like arrows in the hand of a warrior. As women warriors in a spiritual battle, through our prayers and godly example we can shoot the "arrows" of our biological and spiritual children far into the future to win battles for God's Kingdom!

---

19 Chris Taylor, original composition.

In the same way, the sacrifices of our sufferings for Jesus will bear much fruit, not only in our lifetime, but as following generations take courage from our example, they will serve to advance the kingdom of God, bearing 30, 60, and even 100 times more fruit!

NEXT GENERATION BLESSING

We would like to end this book with a Next Generation Blessing Prayer. Please feel free to personalize this prayer for your biological and/or spiritual children, grandchildren, and those yet to be born!

Dear Father,

We pray a blessing on the generations to follow us. We pray that they will come to know You at a very young age. We pray they will love You and serve You all the days of their lives. We pray that they will grow in wisdom and stature and favor with God and man, just like Jesus did.

We pray that they will tell the next generation of Your praiseworthy deeds, Your power, and the wonders You have done. We pray that they would teach their children Your mighty acts, so the next generation would know about them, even the children yet to be born, and they in turn would tell their children. We pray that they would put their trust in You and would not forget Your deeds but keep Your commands.

We pray that when they face trials in life, they will remember that the sufferings they experience in this life are nothing compared to the glory that will be revealed in the next one. We pray that they will stand side by side with us in Heaven praising You for the way that You brought us through, all the while changing us from glory to glory. And we pray that they will not come alone, but through faith in Christ, will bring many untold numbers of people to Heaven with them.

In Jesus' name, Amen.[20]

Take Heart!!

---

20   Mary Beth Woll, MA, LMHC, Linda Smith, and Paul Meier MD, *Don't Lose Heart! A Widow's Guide To Growing Stronger* (The Widows Project, 2020), p. 99-100.

DISCUSSION QUESTIONS

1. Proverbs 13:22 says, "A good man leaves an inheritance to his children's children." In this case, we are not just referring to a material inheritance, but a legacy of godliness which will bless generations after us, even those who are yet to be born! It's amazing to think about the impact of our daily lives on so many others. Reflect on what your parents and grandparents have passed on to you. What do you want to pass on to your children and grandchildren?

    _____

    _____

    _____

    _____

    _____

    _____

    _____

    _____

    _____

    _____

    _____

2. What about the legacy of those who have never had children? How can they leave an inheritance to the generations to come? If you are not a parent at this time, how would you like to live your life in such a way as to impact future generations?

    _____

    _____

    _____

    _____

    _____

_____

_____

_____

_____

_____

_____

_____

3. Although we admire heroes of the faith in our culture, none of them were perfect! We do not have to live perfect lives to impact those who follow us. In fact, some of us may best glorify God by telling of His wonderful forgiveness and restoration in our lives, or how He saved us from calamity and disaster. Consider writing a letter to your children, grandchildren, or others your life may have touched, to tell them what God has done to help you through the loss of your wife. What is the legacy you would most want to impart to them?

_____

_____

_____

_____

_____

_____

_____

_____

_____

_____

_____

_____

Twelve Growing Stronger Guidelines

1. **Keep First Things First.**
   Develop an intimate relationship with Jesus, the true Higher Power because you are powerless to overcome crises in your own strength alone. "The Spirit of the Sovereign Lord is on me, because the Lord has anointed me to preach good news to the poor" (Isaiah 61:1).

2. **Balance Suffering In Communion and Community.**
   Give your broken heart to God and His people to receive healing from both. "The Spirit of the Sovereign Lord is on me . . . He has sent me to bind up the brokenhearted" (Isaiah 61:1).

3. **Connection Leads to Freedom.**
   To become truly free from bondage and truly healed, you must confess your own sins and flaws to safe significant others as well as to Jesus. "The Spirit of the Sovereign Lord is on me . . . to proclaim freedom for the captives and release from darkness for the prisoners" (Isaiah 61:1).

4. **Throw Off What Hinders.**
   With God's help, get rid of it. Lay aside the things that are holding you back. "Therefore, since we are surrounded by such a great cloud of witnesses, let us throw off everything that hinders and the sin that so easily entangles, and let us run with perseverance the race marked out for us" (Hebrews 12:1).

5. **Keep Looking Up.**
   Make personal growth an even higher priority than resolving your current crisis. "Let us fix our eyes on Jesus, the author and perfector of our faith" (Hebrews 12:2a).

6. **Stand Strong.**
   Whenever you feel like giving up, endure. "Jesus . . . for the joy set before Him endured the cross, scorning its shame, and sat down at the right hand of the throne of God" (Hebrews 12:2b).

7. **TAKE HEART!**
   When you experience discipline, remind yourself that God is a good Father and say, "My Abba (Daddy) Father loves me." "Moreover, we have all had human fathers who disciplined us, and we respected them for it. How much more should we submit to the Father of our spirits and live!" (Hebrews 12:10).

8. **RUN YOUR RACE.**
   Remember, your victory is just around the corner. "Therefore, strengthen your feeble arms and weak knees. Make level paths for your feet, so that the lame may not be disabled, but rather healed" (Hebrews 12:12–13).

9. **REMEMBER THAT GOD IS ON YOUR SIDE.**
   God's love is based on His love for you, not on your performance. "The Spirit of the Lord is on me . . . to proclaim the year of the Lord's favor and the day of vengeance of our God" (Isaiah 61:1a-2).

10. **GRIEVE WITH COMPANY.**
   Weep with those who weep until God wipes away all your tears. "The Spirit of the Lord is on me . . . to comfort all who mourn, and provide for those who grieve in Zion—to bestow on them a crown of beauty instead of ashes, the oil of gladness instead of mourning, and a garment of praise instead of a spirit of despair" (Isaiah 61:1a,2b–3).

11. **LET YOUR LIGHT SHINE.**
   Grow stronger through your loss and become a blessing to others. "They will be called oaks of righteousness, a planting of the Lord for the display of His splendor" (Isaiah 61:3b).

12. **LEAVE A LEGACY.**
   When you glorify God through your grief, you become an example that will encourage generations to come. "They will rebuild the ancient ruins and restore the places long devastated; they will renew the ruined cities that have been devastated for generations" (Isaiah 61:4).

How to Find a Great Therapist
By Mary Beth Woll, MA, LMHC

"Wait a second! Find a therapist?!? Do I need therapy? With a little willpower, I could handle this on my own, right?"

The truth is, everybody needs counsel, at one time or another, from loved ones, trusted family and friends, pastors, mentors, and professionals. Taking this important step could save a person's life and potentially change the course of many generations to come!

Before beginning the search for a therapist, it is good to clearly define the need.

- What are my symptoms?
- Is there an immediate threat to someone's safety?
- Is there a desire to include spirituality in therapy?
- Will it be individual, group, or family therapy?
- Is there a need for a specialist in treating such cases as bipolar disorder, post-traumatic stress disorder, and others?
- How will I pay for it? Can I use my insurance? (Currently, children are covered under their parent's insurance until age 26, even if married.) Do they offer a sliding scale?
- Would a support group or peer counseling provide what I need, or do I need a professional who specializes in my situation?

With all these questions, is it any wonder that many people never make it to the therapist's door? There are good answers to all these questions, but even before answering them, there are often other roadblocks that need to be addressed, like how does one even know when it's time to see a professional?

How can I determine if I need therapy?

Consider when a person catches a cold. If they are sensible, they will drink more fluids and get more rest. If the cold persists, they may take vitamins or over-the-counter cold remedies. If the cold develops into bronchitis or pneumonia, it's time to see a doctor! In such cases, it would be unwise and potentially life-threatening to continue to self-treat or self-medicate.

In the same way, it is important to recognize when emotional, behavioral, or soul needs are too much for one's personal support system. That's when it's time to stop "white-knuckling it" and get professional help!

AS A CHRISTIAN, SHOULDN'T I JUST RELY ON MY CHURCH AND MY FAITH INSTEAD OF A COUNSELOR?

Sometimes a person's faith background or the religious traditions they were brought up with can be a roadblock toward counseling. Many have been taught that if their faith is strong enough, they need not rely on outside counseling. Some wonder, "Is it even okay for a Christian to go to therapy? If I were a 'better Christian,' I wouldn't need therapy, right? Shouldn't I just read my Bible and pray more?"

This kind of thinking can prolong a person's pain and unnecessarily add to the shame they may already be experiencing. If someone is dealing with past trauma or abuse, some kind of addiction, or any number of other mental health challenges, a trained counselor can be an incredible tool and ally. In these cases, telling them, "You don't need counseling. Just become a better, stronger Christian," or "Just read the Bible and pray more," can condemn them to more years of symptoms, hiding, and unhealthy coping strategies instead of being helpful. In a loving community of faith, we really should be encouraging each other to seek out the help we need, and receiving help from a trained counselor is a wonderful and healthy avenue.

WHAT ABOUT MEDICATION?

Sometimes, there is a very real and legitimate need for medication in treatment for depression, anxiety, and bipolar disorder, among others. This must not be minimized any more than one would advise a diabetic not to take their insulin! Often people struggle with the idea of starting on medication, thinking that it makes them seem weak or even "crazy." The reality is that the brain is an organ, like any other part of the body, which can become sick. In some cases, the brain is formed a little differently from birth and requires medical support.

Many Christians, and particularly those who have overcome drug addiction, struggle with medication issues, thinking that a "better Christian" would not need an antidepressant or mood stabilizer. This misconception can keep many people away from much-needed treatment. Of course, it is true that God still heals miraculously, but He can also choose to use medicine to heal us, and does not condemn us for it. Jesus confirmed this when He said in Matthew 9:12, "It is not those who are healthy who need a physician, but those who are sick." Praying for the sick is a vital ministry of the church, but it is just as dangerous for the church to advise against medicine as it would be for pastors and church members to line up and write out prescriptions for each other on Sunday mornings! This calls for a mental health professional.

Although therapists do not prescribe medicine, they can diagnose and refer for proper medical treatment, which is most effective in conjunction with therapy.

IS MY PAST AFFECTING MY CURRENT LIFE AND RELATIONSHIPS?

Some people experience childhood sexual abuse or other trauma that is terrifying or impossible for a child to understand. Memories of such horror don't go away. They are so threatening that the mind could protect the person by locking these memories away in the subconscious for years while the person carries on with the business of growing up. Later, these memories can present as unexplained behavioral symptoms or big blank blocks of time in their childhood memories. When these symptoms begin to emerge in adult years, the person may need someone who can help them articulate and resolve what was previously unspeakable.

When they are ready to face the pain of the past, it is not safe or appropriate to talk to just anyone, although friends and family may play a part in the healing process. It is important that they seek out someone who is trained and skilled in such work; otherwise, it is possible for the unequipped helper to inflict more damage in the process.

HOW CAN COUNSELING HELP MY RELATIONSHIPS?

In addition to depression, post-traumatic symptoms and anxiety, relationships may become so conflicted or distant that a third party's perspective and input is needed. Such situations can be overwhelming to a widow's support system of friends and family. Once again, professional help is in order. Seeking counseling in such cases is actually the responsible thing to do in order to continue to function well in the family and on the job.

WHAT TYPE OF THERAPIST IS BEST FOR ME?

Some of the confusion in finding a great therapist can be found in the titles alone.

- Psychiatrists will usually be identified as "Dr." with "MD" following their name. These medical doctors specialize in the diagnosis and treatment of mental or psychiatric illnesses. They are trained in counseling, but typically use the client's report of symptoms to prescribe appropriate medications and refer clients to therapists for counseling. While it is true that family practice doctors prescribe the overwhelming proportion of antidepressants in the United States, I prefer to recommend a psychiatrist when medication is needed because, as specialists, they can often catch a subtle need that can make a big difference in prescribing the right medication.

- Psychologists (PhD or PsyD) have a doctoral degree in psychology. They are specialists in various methods of therapy, as well as psychological testing. Psychologists do not prescribe medications but can refer to a psychiatrist, if necessary.

- Licensed Mental Health Counselors (LMHC, LCPC) have a master's degree in psychology, plus 3,000 hours of post-master's experience in order to be licensed. They are therapists who can diagnose and treat a wide range of problems including depression, anxiety, bipolar disorder, post-traumatic stress disorder (PTSD), sexual abuse, ADD/ADHD, grief, suicidal impulses, addiction, substance abuse, stress management, self-esteem issues, emotional health and family, parenting and marital issues. In addition to individuals, they can treat couples and families. They do not prescribe medications but can refer to a psychiatrist.

- Licensed Marriage and Family Therapists, (LMFT) are therapists with a master's degree in psychology and post-master's experience (similar to the Licensed Mental Health Counselor) but with more specialized training in issues regarding marriage and family. They can also treat all the issues listed above.

- Licensed Social Workers (MSW, LCSW) also have a master's degree in social work and post-master's experience. They specialize in providing services to help their clients' psychological and social functioning. Social workers can also treat the above therapy issues. In addition, they are specially trained to provide counseling and resources to help a person better function in their environment and relationships.

- Pastoral Counselors (Rev., MDiv, Pastor) are usually licensed or ordained ministers who also have training in counseling. Their emphasis tends to focus on biblical principles, spiritual formation and direction, and improving relationships. It is important to note that, depending on how or where the pastor was ordained, they may not have been required to have any training in counseling at all. It is dangerous to assume that just because someone is a pastor, they are equipped to provide counsel in areas of mental health.

(NOTE: States have similar licenses but may use different license names/initials and may have different requirements. For example, a Licensed Mental Health Counselor (LMHC) in the State of Washington is similar to a Licensed Clinical Professional Counselor (LCPC) in the State of Illinois, but there may be some differences. Don't hesitate to ask for clarification of the initials or degree of a professional when scheduling to see them.)

HOW CAN I DETERMINE I'VE FOUND THE RIGHT THERAPIST FOR ME?

In an effort to answer some of these concerns, I will share how I found my own therapist. Yes, therapists need therapists too! We all have injuries in life. The better healed I am, the better therapist I will be. Experiencing the process also gives me empathy for my clients who are undergoing this process.

Here are the things that were important to me as I looked for a therapist:

- **Covered**: She was listed on my insurance plan.
- **Competence**: She went to a respected university and has a good work history.
- **Conviction**: There are certain moral principles which are non-negotiable for me. I didn't want to wrestle with these issues during therapy but needed someone who shared this baseline with me so they would be better able to advise me. Since my faith informs my decisions, choosing a therapist who was also a Christian was *the* most important aspect for

me.

- **Compassion**: I found that she is a very caring individual. This is also critical for me. If I felt that the therapist didn't really care, I would go elsewhere.
- **Connection**: She and I "hit it off." This makes therapy so much more pleasant.
- **Consistency**: She is dependable and reliable. I know what to expect when I go to therapy.
- **Convenience**: Her office is within about a half hour commute. I was willing to travel this distance for a great therapist.

Finding a great therapist has been a huge benefit in my own life. Hopefully, these thoughts will also help you navigate the maze of finding a therapist who is a good fit for you. As a counselor, I know that I have the opportunity to change lives daily! Sometimes, like braces, it is slow and incremental. Other times, like heart surgery, it is critical and immediate. Still for others it is like physical therapy— just plain hard work, long-term, and endurance-building.

It takes courage to begin the counseling process. Often, we will experience resistance from within ourselves and from others. This is normal and to be expected. But the rewards are well worth the risk as these life changes can be deep, permanent, and enriching not only for you, but for your loved ones. And even one changed life can change the course of events for generations yet to come!

NEXT GENERATION BLESSING

Next Generation Blessing

Dear Father,

We pray a blessing on the generations to follow us. We pray that they will come to know You at a very young age. We pray they will love You and serve You all the days of their lives. We pray that they will grow in wisdom and stature and favor with God and man, just like Jesus did.

We pray that they will tell the next generation of Your praiseworthy deeds, Your power, and the wonders You have done. We pray that they would teach their children Your mighty acts, so the next generation would know about them, even the children yet to be born, and they in turn would tell their children. We pray that they would put their trust in You and would not forget Your deeds but keep Your commands.

We pray that when they face trials in life, they will remember that the sufferings they experience in this life are nothing compared to the glory that will be revealed in the next one. We pray that they will stand side by side with us in Heaven praising You for the way that You brought us through, all the while changing us from glory to glory. And we pray that they will not come alone, but through faith in Christ, will bring many untold numbers of people to Heaven with them.

In Jesus' name, Amen.

RESOURCES

QUIET TIME
Sarah Young, *Jesus Calling: Enjoying Peace in His Presence* (Nashville, Thomas Nelson Publishers, 2004, 2011, 2012, 2013).

Worthy Inspired, *Overcoming Tough Times: God's Answer to Every Situation (New York:* Worthy Publishing, 2016).

Donna Fagerstrom, *Every Mourning* (MPACT Communications, 2017).

Donna Fagerstrom, *Cada Mañana (MPACT Communications).*

Ken and Jeanne Harrington, *From Curses to Blessings: Removing Generational Curses (*Shippensburg, PA: Destiny Image Publishers, 2011).

John and Stasi Eldredge, *Love and War: Finding the Marriage You've Dreamed Of* (New York: Doubleday, 2009), p. 213.

WALKIE-TALKIE ROTE PRAYERS
This first one is adapted from a daily prayer in *From Curses to Blessings: Removing Generational Curses* by Ken and Jeanne Harrington.[21]

Jesus, my best friend, I agree with You that today, together, we will separate me from any hindrance, any spiritual stronghold, anything You set Your attention on, that separates me from Your vision, power and courage for my life. What separates me from You right now? Selah (pause and listen/look for His answer). What do You want me to get about vision, power or courage for my life? Selah. I give You permission to separate the chaff from my life. What is life and what is chaff for me today? Selah.

God, by trusting You, I am grafted into You (meditate on "grafted into God") and into Abraham. I call from heaven the promises and the power to prosper that You gave Abraham. What does that look like for me today? Selah. I receive the world and all that is in it as my inheritance.

---

21   Ken and Jeanne Harrington, F*rom Curses to Blessings: Removing Generational Curses (*Shippensburg, PA: Destiny Image Publishers, 2011).

God, give me integrity to be a good manager of all You trust me with today. What are You trusting me with today, Lord? Empower me to live into the destiny that you purposed, planned and put it in action for me before I was even conceived. Open the heavens that I may receive vision, provision, and power from You to do that. What does that look like for me today and what does my destiny have to do with today? Selah. I agree with You that I will expand Your Kingdom and bring honor and love to You the rest of my life. I agree with You that Your Spirit will so transform my heart that I know intimately my Daddy's amazingly huge love for me and have trust to receive what You would give me. What do You want to give me today? Selah. I declare that You are good, God, so good!

Right now, I purpose to go after all that belongs to me today. What belongs to me today? Selah. I agree with You, in Jesus' name, that all the gifts, the callings, the talents, the abilities, the lost inheritances, the influence, and the creativity that belong to me, will pass down to me from the generations before. I agree with You that I will transmit all of that to the generations that follow me. What might that reception and transmission look like to You for me today? Selah.

Thank You, God that through changing my way of thinking and canceling the debt of love that I owed You, You have removed and are removing blockages that have kept me from receiving the rest of Your gifts to me. I agree with You that those gifts will overtake me and run me down. I agree with You that I will stop whatever I'm busy at and receive them when they show up. I agree with You that I will truly depart from my mistakes in action, my mistaken mindsets, and receive Your power for my life in exchange. What does this look like for me today? What exchange would You like to make with me? Selah.

I bow my heart to my best friend, Jesus' Daddy. I agree with You that You transmit strength through the power of Your Spirit to my inner self, so Jesus will live more fully in my heart through trust. Being rooted and grounded in His love, I will comprehend with others, the width and length and depth and height of Your love. I'll know Jesus' love by experience, not just in my head. I agree with You that I will be filled with all the fullness of Jesus. How does that look to You for me today? Selah.

Now to You who are able to do exceedingly, abundantly above all that I ask or think, according to Your power that works in me, to You be magnificent and powerful celebrations of honor and love. I, together with Your followers, glorify You, Jesus. You keep Your promises to all generations forever and ever.

I'm in!

§

This next one is based on the daily prayer in John and Stasi Eldredge's book, *Love and War: Finding the Marriage You've Dreamed Of.*[22]

Lord Jesus, I give You my home, my family, and the rest of my relationships. Cover us with Your life and fill us with Your life. Come and be the Lord of my home, my family and my other relationships.

My dear Lord Jesus, I come to You now to be restored in You, to be renewed in You, to receive Your love, Your life, and all the mercy and power to become what I am not, that I so desperately need this day. I honor You as my sovereign Lord, and I surrender every aspect of my life totally and completely to You. I give You my spirit, soul, and body; my heart, mind, and will. I cover myself with Your life—my spirit, soul, and body; my heart, mind, and will. I ask Your Holy Spirit to restore me in You, renew me in You, and lead me in this time of talking with You. How do You want to do that? Selah. In all that I now say, I stand in total agreement with Your Spirit.

In all that I now ask, I include my children, their spouses, and their children. Acting as their head, I bring them under Your authority and covering as I come under Your authority and covering.

I cover my kids, their spouses and our grandkids (I name each individually) with Your life—their spirits, souls, and bodies; their hearts, minds, and wills. I ask Your Spirit to restore them in You, renew them in You, and apply to them all that I now ask on their behalf, acting as their head.

---

22   John and Stasi Eldredge, *Love and War: Finding the Marriage You've Dreamed Of* (New York: Doubleday, 2009), p. 213.

Dear God, holy and victorious Trinity, You alone are worthy of all my worship, my heart's devotion, all my praise, all my trust, and all the beauty and impact of my life. I love You, I worship You, I trust You. I give myself over to You in my heart's search for life. You alone are life, and You have become my life. I renounce all other gods, all idols, and I give You the place in my heart and in my life that You truly deserve. How can I best do that today, God? Selah. I confess here and now that this is all about You, God, and not about me. You are the hero of this story, and I belong to You. Forgive me for my every mistake. Search me and know me and reveal to me where You are working in my life. Where are You working in my life? Selah. Please grant me the power to become what I'm not through Your healing, deliverance, and a deep and true change in my way of thinking.

Dear Daddy, thank You for loving me and choosing me before You made the world. You are my true Father—my Creator, Redeemer, Sustainer, and the true end of all things, including my life. I love You, I trust You, I worship You. I give myself over to You to be one with You in all things, as Jesus is one with You. What does that look like for me today? Selah. Thank You for proving Your love for me by sending Jesus. I receive Him and all His life and all His work, which You purposed, planned, and put in action for me before I was even conceived. Thank You for including me in the promise, for forgiving me my mistakes, for granting me His right standing with You, for making me complete in Him. Thank You for making me alive with the promise, raising me with Him, seating me with Him at Your right hand, establishing me in His authority, and covering and filling me with Your Holy Spirit, Your love, and Your favor. I receive it all with thanks and give it total claim to my life—my spirit, soul, and body; my heart, mind, and will. I bring the life and work of Jesus over my children, their spouses and their children, and over my home, my household, my vehicles, finances, all my kingdom and domain.

Jesus, thank You for coming to ransom me with Your own life. I love You, I worship You, I trust You. I give myself over to You, to be one with You in all things. And I receive all the work and all of the triumph of Your cross, death, life, and sacrifice for me, through which I am atoned. I am ransomed and transferred to Your kingdom, my sin-making nature is removed, my heart is set apart to and for You, and every claim made against me is disarmed this day. I now take my place in Your cross and death, through which I have died with You to my sin, to my flesh, to the world, and to the evil one. I take up the cross and crucify my flesh with all its pride, arrogance, unbelief, and idolatry (including anything I'm currently struggling with—like anxious churning thoughts). I put off the old man. I ask You to apply to me the fullness of Your cross, death, life, and sacrifice. What do You want that to look like for me today? Selah. I receive it with thanks and give it total claim to my spirit, soul, and body, and my heart, mind, and will.

Jesus, I also sincerely receive You as my life, my holiness, and my strength. I receive all the work and triumph of Your resurrection, through which You have conquered sin, and death, and judgment. Death has no mastery over You, nor does any foul thing. And I have been raised with You to a new life, to live Your life—dead to sin and alive to You, Jesus. I now take my place in Your resurrection and in Your life, through which I am saved by Your life. How do You want me to do that today? Selah. I reign in life through Your life. How do I do that today? Selah. I receive Your life—Your humility, love and forgiveness, Your integrity, wisdom, strength, joy, and Your union with the Father. How do I do that today? Selah. Apply to me the fullness of Your resurrection. I receive it with thanks and give it total claim to my spirit, soul, and body, and my heart, mind, and will.

Jesus, I also sincerely receive You as my authority, rule, and dominion, my everlasting victory against Satan and his kingdom, and my ability to bring Your kingdom at all times and in every way. How do I do that today? Selah. I receive all the work and triumph of Your ascension, through which You have judged Satan and cast him down. You have disarmed his kingdom. All authority in heaven and on earth is given to You, Jesus. I now take my place in Your ascension, and Your throne, through which I have been raised with You to the right hand of the Father and established in Your authority. What does that look like for me today, Jesus? Selah. I now bring the kingdom of God and the authority, rule, and dominion of Jesus, my promise, over my life today, over my family, my home, my household, my vehicles, and finances—over all my kingdom and domain.

I now bring Your authority, rule, and dominion, Lord Jesus, my promise, and the fullness of the work of that promise, against Satan, against his kingdom, against every foul and unclean spirit that is against me. I specifically bring it against the spirit of rebellion, which causes me to attempt to be my own salvation. (Name the specific battles and enemies I know have been attacking me.) I bring Your full work, Jesus, against every foul power and black art. I bind it all from me in Your authority and in Your name. I also place Your cross between me and all people, so that only Your love may pass between us.

Holy Spirit, thank You for coming. I love You, I worship You, I trust You. I sincerely receive You and all the work and victory in Pentecost, through which You have come. You have clothed me with power from on high and sealed me in the promise. You have become my union with the Father and the Son, become the Spirit of Truth in me, the life of God in me, my Counselor, Comforter, Strength, and Guide. I honor You as my Sovereign, and I yield every dimension of my life to You, and You alone, to be filled with You and to walk in step with You in all things. Fill me up once again. Restore my union with the Father and the Son. Lead me in all truth, cover and fill me for all my life and walk and calling, and lead me deeper into Jesus today. I receive You with thanks, and I give You total claim to my life.

Heavenly Father, thank You for granting me every spiritual blessing in Jesus. I claim the riches in You, my promise, Jesus, over my life today. I bring the life of my promise over my spirit, soul, and body, my heart, mind, and will. I put on the full armor of God—the belt of truth, breastplate of righteousness, shoes of readiness with the good news of peace, and the helmet of salvation. I take up the shield of faith, the sword of Your Word and the weapon of prayer. I choose to wield these weapons at all times in Your power, God. I choose to talk with You at all times in spirit and in truth.

Thank You for Your angels. I ask for their help and protection this day, and I ask that they establish Your kingdom throughout my kingdom and domain. I now call forth Your kingdom, Jesus, my promise, throughout my home, my family, my kingdom, and my domain, in Your name and authority O Lord Jesus, my promise, with all glory and honor and thanks to You.

SCRIPTURES FOR MEDITATION
(BRUCE'S PERSONALIZED VERSION)

Here are some of my favorites since Cheri passed. I hope one or more of them will resonate with you and you'll try the meditation technique described in Chapter 1.

You are the One who goes before me, and You stay with me and hold onto me. I will be brave and encouraged, God (Deuteronomy 31:8, HCSB).

I trust You, Jesus, for You have paid off all my debts. You have summoned me by name; I am Yours, Jesus (Isaiah 43:1, MSG).

Since I am living in the light, I have fellowship with You, God. And Your life, Jesus, cleanses me from all my mistakes and guilt and their manifestations in my life (1 John 1:7 NLT, AMP).

I am always calm and focused, for in everything, by prayer and petition, with thanks, I present my requests to You, God. And Your peace, Jesus my promise, which transcends my understanding, guards my heart and mind (Philippians 4:6–7).

I fix my thoughts on what is true and honorable and right and pure and lovely and admirable. I think about things that are excellent and worthy of praise (Philippians 4:8, NLT).

Jesus, I devote myself to talking with You with an alert mind and a thankful heart (Colossians 4:2, NLT).

Yea, though I walk through the valley of the shadow of death, I fear no evil, for You are with me, Jesus. Your rod and Your staff, they comfort me (Psalm 23:4, NKJV).

I trust You, Jesus, my promise, and I find new strength. I soar high on wings like an eagle. I run and do not grow weary. I walk and do not faint (Isaiah 40:31, NLT).

I wait for You, Jesus. My whole being waits, and in Your Word, I put my hope. (Psalm 130:5).

Jesus, my God right here—my Mighty One—You save me. You freak out over me with gladness. You quiet me with your love. You sing out over me with joy (Zepheniah 3:17, NKJV).

You keep me in perfect peace because I trust in You, Jesus, because my thoughts are fixed on You! (Isaiah 26:3, NLT).

You wipe every tear from my eyes, Jesus. There will be no more death or mourning or crying or pain, for the old order of things has passed away. (Revelation 21:4).

You renew hope, Jesus! And You heal my body (Psalm 147:3, CEV).

You are my refuge and my strength, Lord. You are my ever-present help in trouble (Psalm 46:1).

I cry to You for help when my heart is overwhelmed, Jesus, and You lead me to the towering rock of safety (Psalm 61:2b, NLT).

You are close to me when I am brokenhearted, Jesus. You save me when I am crushed in spirit (Psalm 34:18).

God sent You to comfort me when I mourn, Jesus. He sent You to give me flowers in place of my sorrow, olive oil in place of my tears, and joyous praise in place of my broken heart (Isaiah 61:2-3, CEV).

You have upheld me since my birth and have carried me since I was born. Even to my old age and gray hairs You are He. You are He who sustains me, Lord. You made me, and you carry me; You sustain me, and You rescue me (Isaiah 46:3–4).

Oh, Jesus, You are my Lord; I earnestly search for You. My soul thirsts for You; my whole body longs for You in this parched and weary land where there is no water (Psalm 63:1, NLT).

I come to You when I am weary and burdened, and You give me rest, Jesus. I take up Your yoke and learn from You, because You are gentle and humble in heart, and I find rest for my mind, will and emotions (Matthew 11:28–29, NKJV).

You are my strength and my song; You have become my safety, God (Exoduis 15:2, HCSB).

Your instructions are perfect, God, reviving my soul. Your commandments are right, bringing joy to my heart. Your commands are clear, giving me insight for living (Psalm 19:7–8, NLT).

I am always with You, Lord. You hold me by my right hand. You guide me with your counsel, and afterward You will take me to live with You in Your glory (Psalm 73:23–24).

You have given me a new heart, Lord, and You put a new spirit within me. You have removed my heart of stone and given me a heart of flesh (Ezekiel 36:26, HCSB).

All goes well with me, and I am in good health, as all goes well with my soul (3 John 1:2, ESV).

I prosper in every way, and I am in good health physically just as I am spiritually (3 John 1:2, HCSB).

You are with me when I pass through the waters, Jesus; and when I pass through the rivers, they do not overwhelm me. I am not scorched when I walk through the fire, and the flame does not burn me (Isaiah 43:2, HCSB).

Lord, You said, "You make me wise and show me where to go. You guide me and watch over me" (Psalm 32:8, NCV).

You take care of me, Lord, when I stay close to You (Psalm 31:23a, MSG).

When I delight in You, You delight in my way. You make my steps firm. Though I may stumble, Jesus, I always walk tall, for You hold me up with your hand (Psalm 37:23–24).

You give me strength when I'm weary, Jesus. You give me power when I am weak (Isaiah 40:28).

Jesus, my promise, You are my hiding place; You protect me from trouble. You surround me with victory songs (pause and reflect). You guide me along the best pathway for my life. You advise me and watch over me, Lord (Psalm 32:7–8, NLT).
I leave inexperience behind and I live; I pursue the way of understanding (Proverbs 9:6, HCSB).

I can receive bad news calmly, God. I confidently trust You to care for me. I am fearless; I face my foes triumphantly (Psalm 112:7–8, NLT).

I trust You at all times; I pour out my heart to You; You are my refuge, Lord (Psalm 62:8).

This is what I feel you say to me: "Only in returning to You— resting in You—is safety. In quietness and confidence in You is strength, Lord" (Isaiah 30:15, NLT).

In Your light, I see light, Lord; for with You is the fountain of life (Psalm 39:6).

I love You, and I am in awe of You. You show me the path to choose, Lord. I live in prosperity and my children inherit the promise (Psalm 25:12–13, NLT).

You rewrote the text of my life, God, when I opened the book of my heart to Your eyes (Psalm 18:24, MSG).

Ever since the world was created, people have seen the earth and sky. Through everything You made, Lord, I can clearly see Your invisible qualities—Your eternal power and divine nature, so I have no excuse for not knowing You (Romans 1:20, NLT).

I sought You, Lord, and You answered me; You delivered me from all my fears. When I look to You, I am radiant; my face is never covered with shame. This poor man called, and You heard me; You saved me out of all my troubles (Psalm 34:4–6).

This, Lord, is my comfort and consolation in affliction: that Your Word has revived me and given me life. (Psalm 119:50, AMPC).

Restoration for the Soul

Transformation Prayer Ministry (TPM)

This is a facilitated style of prayer that brings healing to wounded parts of the soul—the mind, will, and emotions. You can learn about it at *www.transformationprayer.org.*

I (Bruce) have had TPM sessions regularly for many years, much more so since Cheri passed. They have done much to heal my broken heart. They bring Jesus' comfort and counsel to the deep hurting places of my soul. I am truly a different person—more peaceful, compassionate, and purposeful as a result.

The sessions can be in-person with a facilitator (Chris Taylor is one of these). They can also be done remotely using telephone or internet to connect the facilitator and participant. Chris' website is *www.candlelightministries.net.*

My friend Neil Harmsworth is also a TPM facilitator who specializes in working with leaders in Christian work. You can find out more about Neil at *www.neilharmsworth.com.*

Family Foundations International (FFI)

Seminars, books and recordings on a variety of family issues ranging from relationships to finances. In the United States, see *www.familyfoundations.com.*

For Spanish books and recordings, it's best to contact the FFI Colombia office:

> *https://fundamentosparalafamilia.org/*
> info@fundamentosparalafamilia.org
> Teléfono: (571) 3551550

For Seminars in Spanish information, contact the FFI home office:

> info@familyfoundations.com
> or call 1.303.797.1139.

For French resources, FFI Canada is the source.

> *https://www.familyfoundations.ca/*
> Phone: 403.720.6772
> Email: canada@familyfoundations.ca

OUTREACH TOOLS

The Grief Journey is a series of four encouraging and very helpful books designed to be given to a widowed person at specific times during the first year after their loss. Available from Stephen Ministries. Learn more at:

https://www.stephenministries.org/default.cfm

ABOUT THE AUTHORS

BRUCE MCLEOD was married to Cheri for twenty-three years. They have five children and eight grandchildren. Together, they were singles and youth group leaders. They made three missionary trips to Venezuela; one of those was for a year. The three children still living with them went on that trip. Bruce and Cheri became relational scientists in 2000. In this role, they facilitated seminars, small group studies and individual healing sessions on a variety of family issues. This work continued until Cheri passed away in 2017.

CHRIS TAYLOR was widowed after 38 years of marriage to Irene in 2010. Since 2015 Chris has been married to Carmen and they reside in Everett, Washington. Chris comes with a background of 18 years with Foursquare churches. For several years, Chris was involved with Family Foundations International where he served as an area coordinator. He has been associated with Transformation Prayer Ministry with Dr. Ed Smith for over 20 years and has served as a facilitator with several GriefShare groups. In 2003 Chris formed a nonprofit called Candlelight Ministries dedicated to emotional health and wholeness in the Body of Christ. This ministry continues today with ongoing personal ministry, training and mentoring.

www.ingramcontent.com/pod-product-compliance
Lightning Source LLC
Chambersburg PA
CBHW050725030426
42336CB00012B/1422